The Reset

by Cathal 'Putrid' Haughian

Dedicated to my Mother, my Brothers and Sisters, my Nieces and Nephews and my many Friends.

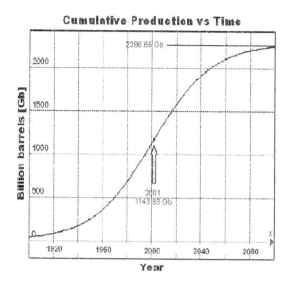

Unfortunately, the world's crude oil depletion state is a little more complicated than the adjacent graph would indicate. This result occurs because all economic activity requires energy to be performed. Since crude oil is used primarily as an energy source, a portion of its energy is needed to produce the oil. Fortunately, three centuries of engineering advancement has provided us with a toolbox of implements for determining what that portion constitutes. They allow us to break down the energy that is in a unit of oil into categories. The graph below shows how the energy in oil **has been**, **is**, and **will be** used.

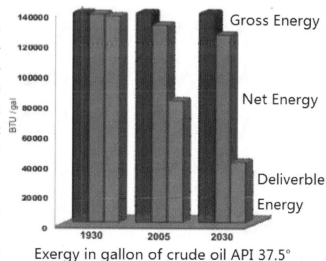

As can be seen from the graph the Deliverable Energy is declining faster than the quantity of crude oil in the reserve. This is not surprising as the Second Law of Thermodynamics informs us that all processes produce irreversibilities, and oil production is a process. The concept of 'irreversibility' can be summed up by the saying "You can't unscramble an egg." When a reservoir of conventional oil is first tapped it is quite orderly; with nicely separated layers of heavy oil, lighter oil, salt water and potable water sitting atop one another. As oil is extracted the elements mix together and the reservoir becomes disordered.

We see this irreversibility production in increasing crude viscosity, increasing well depth, and most of all increasing water cut. The energy to produce our primary energy source, petroleum, is increasing. As it increases the extractable quantity is declining.

The world's crude reserve can be likened to a car battery. As time progresses the battery's internal irreversibilities increase due to entropy production, and we say the battery "gets weak". The internal resistance of the battery increases until the power production of the chemical processes of the battery can no longer overcome the resistance. We say the battery has "gone dead". Like the battery, the internal irreversibilities due to entropy production, of the world's crude oil production system are increasing. The idea of **entropy** comes from a principle of thermodynamics dealing with energy. It usually refers to the idea that everything in the universe eventually moves from order to disorder, and **entropy** is the measurement of that change. Higher viscosity, increasing well depth, and increasing water cut have the same effect as increasing resistance does in the battery.

All processes approach an equilibrium state with their environment. (In similitude, a hot cup of tea will slowly cool to room temperature.) This is called the "dead state", and represents the point where no additional work can be extracted from the system's energy. It is the point where the system's internal irreversibilities overcome the system's energy. The car battery reached the "dead state" when it permanently went "dead". So also will the world's petroleum production system.

The "dead state" can be determined from the fundamental properties of petroleum, its cumulative production history, and a few First and Second Law statements. Once identified it can be used as a benchmark to ascertain the world's crude oil depletion state.

The US is Bleeding Out

If gasoline is the lifeblood of commerce, then the US is bleeding out.

As part of our final analysis of Capitalism the respected BW Hill wrote the following warning against the World War solution:

'The world's petroleum industry has now accumulated $2.5 trillion in debt. That debt is backed primarily by the value of their reserves. Upon becoming apparent that the value of those reserves will rapidly be approaching zero, havoc will break out in the financial sector. There will be $100s of trillions in the derivatives market that will suddenly have no solvent counter party.

Viewing the reported growth in inventory builds, and how much the ETP Model informs us that the inventory must be increasing, we expect this situation to reach a crisis point sometime in 2017 or 2018. It seems highly unlikely that either of the world's nuclear super powers, the US and Russia, will revert to open warfare as a result. Neither would have anything to gain by such action, and much to lose. It does seem likely that the Middle Eastern powers will use the situation as an excuse for attempting to destroying each other. In other words we expect devastation to result for the Middle East.

With the Middle East in flames, and much of their capacity to produce destroyed the world will suddenly see a massive decline in petroleum supplies. Price should increase, but the Maximum Affordability Function informs us that will be short lived. The end result will be that Russia, and a few high quality Western fields will remain as the sole sources for the world's petroleum supply. The economy will be in shambles, and there will be little incentive, and even less means to support wide spread, high tech warfare.'

What does BW Hill mean by the 'Maximum Affordability Function'? The price limit of any good is affordability, if you can't produce at a price potential buyers can bear then you'll make no sales and be bankrupted quite quickly. The maximum price they can bear is determined by their income. And their income is ultimately determined by the amount of net energy gain available to their social group.

The Dominant Class knows this. "But what if your customer has a printing press and can run dual deficits?" I hear you plead. Yes, we know this also, which is why the Government's share of GDP in the US is far larger than in China—a Communist country.

US Governmental and Financial elites have successfully controlled the market since the early 70s via their full spectrum dominance strategy funded by the FIAT—the petrodollar. But as the following charts show; the role of oil is in terminal decline and should no longer play a significant role in the general economy after 2020-2022, if current trends continue. They appear in harmony with predictions put forth in the Hills Group Report. Our concluding analysis explores the result of such for humanity.

Essentially the global market shall collapse when the US loses control of such, which now appears inevitable in the near future. Below are charts supplied by the US Government via the Energy Information Agency. These charts track total gasoline **sales to end users** by US refiners. End users includes bulk consumers, such as agriculture, industry, and utilities, as well as residential and commercial consumers. Data for recent years is being withheld for most states; but the broader picture is quite clear

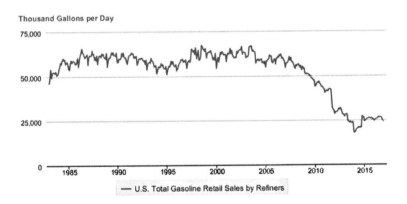

Figures from the East Coast region includes Connecticut, Maine, Massachusetts, Rhode Island, Vermont, Delaware, District of Columbia, Maryland, New Jersey, New York, etc. Some states have fared far better than others, please compare New York to Georgia, New York collapsed in 2014 but somehow recovered:

East Coast (PADD 1) Total Gasoline Retail Sales by Refiners

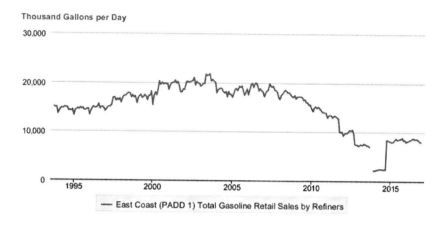

New York hit a peak in May, 2007 at 3,631 thousand gallons per day. The lowest point was 962 thousand gallons in Jan 2014. Then a sudden recovery in Oct 2014. Recent data is 2,490 thousand gallons per day in December 2016.

New York Total Gasoline Retail Sales by Refiners

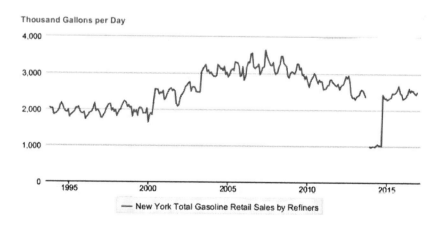

Retail sales by refiners to end use consumers in Georgia hit a peak of 2300 thousand Gallons in Dec 1999, and was 75 thousand gallons in November 2016.

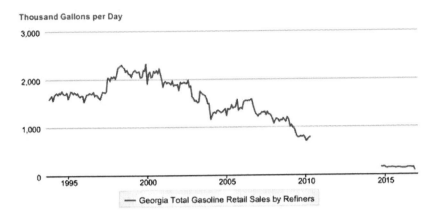

The Midwest region includes the states of Illinois, Indiana, Iowa, Kansas, Kentucky, Michigan, Minnesota, Missouri, Nebraska, Nebraska, Ohio, Oklahoma, South Dakota, Tennessee and Wisconsin. Data by individual state is being withheld:

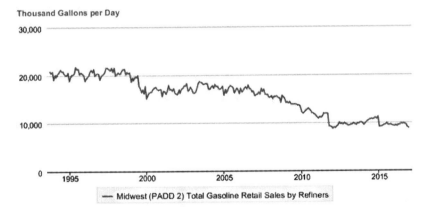

The Gulf Coast Region includes Alabama, Arkansas, Louisiana, Mississippi, New Mexico, Texas and has fallen dangerously. The Gulf Coast region hit a peak of 10,562 thousand gallons per day in Jul 1998. The low point was 496 thousand gallons in Jan 2014.

Gulf Coast (PADD 3) Total Gasoline Retail Sales by Refiners

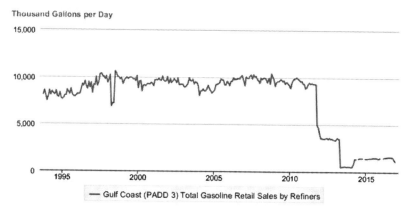

Now you're wondering why the roads aren't all empty. When the refiners realized they were going out of business they sold parts of their retail networks which explains the sharp drop off's in some states. So when we add in bulk sales for the purpose of resale the picture is not so cataclysmic. After crunching the numbers for all grades and formulations—for sales to end users and sales for the purpose of resale—between Jun 2006 and Jun 2016: The total decrease is 16%.

It's possible that production was shifted to candle wax but that's not the case, motor gasoline as a percent of yield is flat at around 45%. (Source, EIA) And sales by volume of other petroleum products are also down (around 4%, EIA). But here's the killer—refinery receipts of crude oil keeps increasing. In 2009 they received 5,261,068 thousand barrels whereas the 2015 figure was 6,004,798 barrels. That's an annualized increase in inputs of 2.2% alongside annualized decrease in sales of 1.45%. Let's call this The End.

U.S. Crude Oil Refinery Receipts

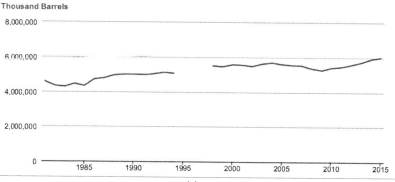

In the words of BW Hill:

The ETP Model is informing us that crude inventories will continue to expand as the petroleum industry's requirement for energy to produce petroleum continues to grow. As a result less energy will be delivered to the non energy producing sector of the economy.'

This is what that looks like:

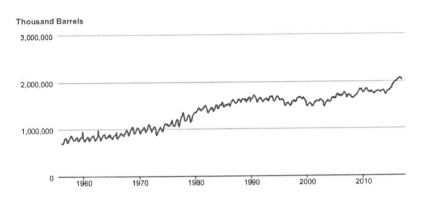

The refineries are the choke point in the system. Even though shale oil production peaked in April 2015, the stock of crude (excluding the strategic reserve which is at 95% capacity) has increased from 326,737 thousand barrels in Mar 2014 to 533,110 barrels in Mar 2017. Please note the rapid and inverse decrease in stocks of finished motor gasoline:

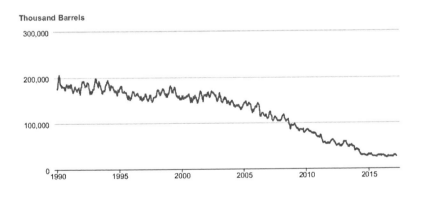

This will result in one of two events occurring:

1) The price will decline until producers can no longer meet the cash flow requirements needed to continue operations; that is, they will then begin to be shut-in.

2) Producers will find that there is insufficient market for their production as inventories reach their maximum affordable level, and will consequently be shut-in.'

In the last analysis, we concentrated on volume of Refinery Receipts and Refinery Sales since such can't be double counted by refinery sub-systems. Having completed the number crunching, and double checked the figures, it appears the model has predictive power.

Central to the model is the Refinery; it would be forced to receive increasingly poor quality inputs (e.g. increasing impurities) as oil fields entered terminal depletion; so an increasing share of such inputs would be discarded, not suited to motor gasoline production, or consumed by the energy intensive refining process; thus the volume of inputs and stock would increase and sales volume decrease. The empirical data confirms these predictions. Since the refineries are receiving more and selling less they can only afford lower crude oil prices unless supported by Federal Reserve Notes aka the petrodollar, AKA IOUs printed by the Fed.

This picture paints the Fed into a very difficult position going forward. Without endless liquidity the Shale Industry would be exposed for the fraud that it is which would undermine support for the Dollar. At the Framework Level, if a company is running at a loss it requires debt, this means one or both of the following statements are true:

1. The company is not competitive with other energy producers

2. The company is not able to add value to inputs purchased

Essentially shale producers are promising to deliver net energy gain to the general economy which simply isn't happening. It doesn't matter how many rigs there are; it doesn't matter how much oil leaves the well head; the only thing that matters is the amount of net energy gain delivered from the Energy

Sector to the general economy. This energy gain is transferred via energy exchange into tools and such which increase productivity, which then increases income. Essentially the Oil Industry in the US is becoming increasingly 'shut-in', in the sense that ever less oil is getting to the population. Now with production from North Dakota in decline lenders shall soon realize the debts can't be repaid. All this while China stockpiles physical Gold—a very difficult situation—to be decided by Imperial Power.

Appendix: Expert meta-analysis by BW Hill

Your charts are very revealing; they indicate what we expect to occur as petroleum loses its capacity to power the economy. That is now occurring at a rate of 1,822 BTU/ gallon, or 76,500 BTU/ barrel per year. To fully appreciate this situation it must be understood that the economy buys energy; only refiners purchase oil. The general user of petroleum products has no reason to buy raw crude. Without adequate processing its value to the economy is essentially zero.

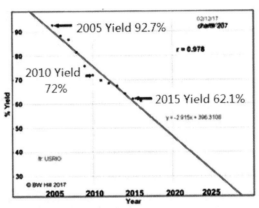

US Refinery Crude Yields Versus Time

The petroleum industry's ability to convert raw crude into a usable finished product is declining rapidly. As shown in the above chart the quantity of crude needed to produce a barrel of finished product has increased by 31% over the last 11 years. In 2005 it required 1.08 barrels of crude to produce a barrel of finished product, by 2015 that had increased to 1.38 barrels. As 85% of a refiner's operating cost is the cost of the crude that they use the price of the crude must decline to compensate for the increasing raw material cost. [Your empirical data suggests annual efficiency losses are presently running at 3.6% for crude oil to motorised gasoline conversion.]

The value of petroleum to the economy is simply its ability to power that economy. The more economic activity it can power the greater its value; the inverse is also true. As the energy in a unit of petroleum is fixed by its molecular structure, the greater the energy requirements to produce it, the less that is available for use to generate economic activity. Over the last 56 years that has fallen by 48%. As petroleum supplies less energy per unit the economy can afford to pay less for it. The economy can pay no more for a unit of petroleum than the amount of economic activity it can power. The economy could not pay $1.14 for oil that can only powered a $1 in economic activity without borrowing the extra 14¢ from somewhere else. That is exactly what is now taking place.

This all relates to the ongoing entropic decay of the Petroleum Production System. Just like an old clock, or an old car it will eventually wear out. The development of the Etp Model was to map the rate of the Production System's entropic decay (wearing out process). The process has now operated through 80% of its maximum theoretical cycle. The theoretical cycle is exactly that; theoretical. Its full life cycle will undoubtedly be less. Somewhere between now, and its maximum the process will stop if left on its own. By our calculations that will require that the world provide $39 trillion by 2030 to keep the process operating. 2030 is its maximum theoretical time line. To keep the process working beyond its 2030 date would require the energy equivalent of 1.62 times all the natural gas produced.

To determine a better estimate than the theoretical one as to when the process will stop we must now look past the Model to more empirical information. We can see it in refinery yields, corporate profits, and an industry that has become so poor that it can not even replace the reserves that it is extracting. Not replacing reserves for an extractive resource industry is an admission that it is going out of business.

Your gasoline usage charts are exactly the kind of high quality empirical data that we are seeking. Thank you for your very valuable contribution.

BW Hill

The Hill's Group

Prepare for Return to the Dark Age

One of the most curious questions in philosophy is what Age we live in presently. What should we call our Age? Did St Aquinas know he lived in the High Middle Age? He lived enlightened by faith in a just society, and can we say our Age is more just than the one he defined? And make no mistake; the Age we knew was the Age of Capital and that Age has ended. With the stroke of my pen I declare it dead.

What Age will follow is the most pressing question; one which the distant past may help answer. Until the Industrial Revolution, there was no measurable growth in output per person. It is a simple economic fact - until the Industrial Revolution economic growth was accounted for by population growth alone. The Industrial Revolution wasn't just enabled by coking coal and the blast furnace—it also required acceptance of a singular idea: usury.

The story of Capitalism is difficult to tell because many of the terms used today were coined in a previous Age when usury was considered unnatural and so severely punished. The evidence of evil was clear to see as bankrupt debtors were known to be imprisoned or killed in unjust societies. Due to such obvious evil and the intellectual output of Aristotle and St Aquinas usury was banned and repressed until the rise of Protestantism let it loose. For these philosophers money was Gold and was not an end but a means of buying goods and services. Putting money out for the generation of more money was considered an evil unto itself.

In the just society desired by St Aquinas there was no profit possible. In a closed economy the **total return** on capital is always zero for everyone's revenue is someone else's cost. (Like how your expenditure is your neighbour's income and vice versa.) Therefore the sum of all revenues equals the sum of all costs and the sum of all return is zero. This is a truism. But for individual agents profits and losses are possible. If there are positive profits for some there are offsetting losses for others so the total sums to zero. And St Aquinas would have considered such arrangement to be just and well for society as an organic whole.

Though the economic implications were profound, if a blacksmith or peasant ran at a loss he would need debt to stay in the game. Though since usury was repressed running at a loss was not possible for very long; so money was not central to economy in the Dark and Middle Ages. And the economy was essentially static.

Thus, the real economy is profitless; though very competitive. This is as true today as it was then. Which is why investors in the real economy don't talk of profit but **return on dollars invested.**

People nowadays have never known anything except work for wages being the main event, so they don't realize that there was a time when that was quite rare. In feudal Europe there were only a few social stations with humans shaped by duties that came with their place. There were peasants, the majority.

The peasants didn't work for wages, they farmed, paid taxes to their lord mainly in kind (chickens, flour, beeswax and so on). There were highly educated aristocrats who lived by taxing the peasants and maintaining law and order. There were craftsmen who were independent or belonged to guilds, and who didn't mostly work for wages—they owned their own shop and tools, and lived from selling their wares. There were people working directly for aristocrats, men at arms, craftspeople, seamstresses, all kinds—but mostly for room and board and clothes and rank-dependent perks; there may have been a bit of money in there somewhere but it wasn't central to the relationship. There were merchants, some of whom eventually turned into capitalists, but they were a tiny minority and the aristocrats stepped on them if they behaved above their station.

What made you important in those days? Not how much money you had. It was how many people you had. If an aristocrat had a lot of gorgeous tapestries it was because he had a lot of farmers paying taxes in flax or wool or such, and in their castle they had a lot of women spinning and weaving and dyeing and embroidering. But your relationship with these farmers and women was not an employment relationship—it was a **permanent** relationship; each side had responsibilities which they could not just terminate on a whim.

So this was not Capitalism. But there were markets and have been such since at least the Bronze Age. Peasants sold some of what they produced at market, and bought things they needed but couldn't produce, as well as luxuries. Craftsmen bought things from peasants and merchants. Merchants traded internationally, guild craftspeople sold some of what they produced to such merchants to be traded internationally. Shippers took loans to get cargo, and so on and so forth. There were obviously markets without Capitalism and capitalists do not require freedom or competition to accumulate capital.

The great myth that deceives many is the notion that capitalism is about markets. It is not. There can be markets without capitalism, and there can be and very often is Capitalism without markets. Current monopolists are far from an anomaly, such things have been common since the Industrial Revolution began.

What Capitalism is about, is **capital**—also wage labour. Capital is anything with exchange or utility value—examples include Gold, silver, land, machines —which is owned by private individuals which can be invested to **rent** labour which adds value to inputs in return for wages. Hopefully, the product gets sold for **more** than the cost of producing it (particularly, for more than the labourers are paid). The product need not be physical, it could be "intellectual property" or financial instruments or whatever has exchange value.

The added value, the **surplus**, is new capital which can be reinvested. Thus, the process is one involving **growth**. And the point of it all is to make the capitalist as rich as possible—for the amount of capital they own to continue growing.

That is Capitalism. Competition is not necessary.

Markets, in the sense of any kind of open opportunity to buy or not buy, are not necessary; monopolistic regulated utilities are still run by capitalists—private individuals who own the capital and seek a return on their investment by paying people to generate it. Defence contractors who "sell" solely to the government based on non-tendered, single-source, cost-plus contracts are also capitalists. The British East India Company, with a crown-granted monopoly on trade with India, was still capitalist.

Owners of privatized for profit prisons—still capitalists.

On the other hand, an economy in which all productive facilities are co-operatives owned by the people who worked at them and which then competed amongst themselves in otherwise familiar "free" markets would **not** be capitalist. A self-sufficient Franciscan monastery was not capitalist.

So the principle of Capitalism is to make as much money as possible by paying workers' wages which are less than the value added by their labour (ideally no more than the minimum they need to survive). Without that difference, that surplus, which the capitalist owns and controls but the workers do not, Capitalism does not exist. Without the capital (such as a factory or web portal) which again the capitalist owns and controls but the workers, the state, feudal nobles and so forth do not, capitalism does not exist.

The Capital is what Capitalism is about.

Capitalists capturing the state and making it do what they want is something which has always been present in real existing Capitalism; you pretty much need a State to pass and enforce Laws to guarantee the process described above. Someone with a gun has to be there to say that banking capitalists can book profit in the present and that the industrial capitalist owns all added-value and workers do not—say by passing laws that dictate commonly owned lands now belong privately to capitalists; thus forcing peasants to abandon their self-sufficient homesteads for the "Satanic Mills".

The internal conflict in the above system is the diametric opposition between Finite Resources and ever increasing Capital and then between wages for Labour and profit for Banking Capitalist and finally return on dollars invested for Real-Economy Capitalist.

Within a system of mass production can the mass consumer (which also happens to be the global labour force) have the buying power to purchase all the goods and services they can produce? Of course not, they need debt to keep the market moving and since they're paid so poorly they've needed a lot of debt since the advent of Neo-Liberalism.

The one who de-constructed Capitalism was Karl Marx in Das Kapital. And because of Marx's definition of "work" the Ordo Liberals of the Freiburg School had to start inventing a new ideology in the 1920's—Neo-Liberalism. What killed Liberalism was the definition between "concrete work" and "abstract work".

- Abstract work = the usual working day/week – 8h/40h.

- Concrete work = all time spent on work that we otherwise would spend on pleasure and social living:
  – 1h lunch

  – 1.5-2h average commuting door to door

  – 0.5h nap because you're exhausted

  – No socializing over at a friend's house on weekdays due to waking up before sunrise, etc…

"Concrete work" thus equals 11-11.5h working day plus further violated "free-time"/lifetime. The polar opposite of your "free-time" is unfree time, and thus work equals slavery by Capitalist definition, which progresses into debt-slavery over the credit cycle. Thus, there's no way Capitalistic Society can reward the labour force fairly or operate as a just society. The Dominant Class have known this for some time:

"As mass production has to be accompanied by mass consumption, mass consumption, in turn, implies a distribution of wealth.....to provide men with buying power. Instead of achieving that kind of distribution, a giant suction pump had by 1929-30 drawn into a few hands an increasing portion of currently produced wealth.....The other fellows could stay in the game only by borrowing. When their credit ran out, the game stopped."

This was written by former Fed Governor Marriner Eccles who was a board member from 1934-51. Is history repeating itself? Why of course it is, were there any changes to the system framework since then? Yes, there actually were, the credit cycle (also known as the business cycle or land price cycle) was removed by the infinite debt potential of the FIAT. Which allowed capital to be privately owned but the debt, dearest, was put on the public book.

So much for understanding Capitalism. And the peasants still support it! And as resources depleted the elite looked to Imperialism for a helping hand. The results have been front page news for decades—war, coup, freedom, fear, terrorist, dictator, IMF, EU, Euro Zone crisis. Sure some of the dumbasses get sacrificed (think martyred) but they don't make the headlines (unless the sycophants require such (think crowd control—9/11 etc.)).

Neither Imperialist nor Capitalist are human-centric rather they are respectively Empire-centric and Capital-centric. A humanoid that is not human-centric is centred on something opposite to human, and is thus by definition anti-human (anti = opposite).

That's the definition of "The Capitalist".

Now an argument must also correspond to the world as we know it, so what is it that makes the world go around? "Growth" and "sustainable growth" not of humans but of capital, the System that rules the world and around which everything revolves is Capitalism and its anti-human consequences are to be seen everywhere.

Most keenly experienced as stress, depression, addiction, separatism, wars, riots and unpayable debt. All of these due to usury.

Most supporters of Capitalism fail to appreciate that all profit is interest and all interest is profit. Interest is profit for the Financial System and it gets divided between those that deposit with the banking system. Invest in banking capital and finally there are bonuses for the bankers for investing their capital and risking your "savings" as well. Be mindful that before Goldman Sachs went public they would risk their own capital which was the norm during the Gold Standard Era.

All growth is enabled by new money issued as interest bearing debt. Recall that the real economy is a zero-sum game so some companies produce less desirable goods than others; the resources of such companies are liquidated via bankruptcy—for they can't service their debts—which is why new money must be issued as interest bearing debt. Additional principal buys additional inputs; the interest represents growth in added value which is confirmed by product purchase. So banking capitalists from the very beginning have enjoyed immense power and wealth as they drive and have developed the tools to capture all growth.

The Rothschild brothers of London writing to associates in New York, 1863:

"The few who understand the system will either be so interested in its profits or be so dependent upon its favours that there will be no opposition from that class, while on the other hand, the great body of people, mentally incapable of comprehending the tremendous advantage that capital derives from the system, will bear its burdens without complaint, and perhaps without even suspecting that the system is inimical to their interests."

They are the dumbasses. And then you get the bullshit—The Protestant Ethic—from the priests who stress hard work, diligence and thrift. (They usually leave out usury and debt-servitude.)

A single transaction economy may aid understanding: 100 dollars lent at 4% buys additional inputs of $100 to produce one additional unit (say an extra wedding cake). The lender books the 4% as $4 profit and seeks to lend this new money into the economy. But if the customer agrees to only pay $101 dollars then there's inflation. Growth in value is 1% but inflation will be around 3% which highlights why growth in output must rise to match the rate of interest. The rate of interest can never be above the rate of growth as investors will park their money (plus debt) in already existing assets which are inflating faster than the rate of growth in the real economy. Why risk your money when you don't need to, right?

So real **output in value** must grow to match the rate of interest, or the rate of interest (aka profit) for the bankers must fall. This puts a check on the financial sector extracting more than they deserve and encourages bankers to allocate money well.

And why is interest bearing debt required to grow output?

There is never enough money **in circulation** to buy the increased product of a growing economy at constant prices. Either prices fall or money must be provided to purchase the additional product. If lent into the economy this money itself demands a future payment as **interest** so the repayment exceeds the initial value loaned. **The lender books the future interest payment as profit in the present.** This is lawful and why all profit is interest and all interest is profit. It also explains why ninja loans were the darling of Wall Street prior to 2007: as they carried sky-high interest rates they also promised more profit (and bonuses) for bankers.

Note also that the money loaned is to pay for the increase and absorption of the additional product. At constant prices this additional product cannot be paid for as the cost of production paid to labour and capital can only cover a value equal to last period's product. There is **not enough money in circulation** to earn the money or real product to cover the loan.

Essentially, the additional real product has been **sold to the lender** who has deferred collection. And in the form of interest is promised a payment for that deferral by the borrower. (That promise isn't so important nowadays since the FIAT lets the banker book the profit in the present and more money can always be printed if the plan goes awry, but during the Gold Standard Era every promise was backed by collateral so investment was allocated very carefully.)

Since the borrower has consumed the additional product there is no way to repay the loan when it comes due. The debt is either repudiated or extended.

If extended there is still no earned money to pay the additional interest so the debt will grow through the issuance of new debt to cover the interest on the unpayable old debt.

Next period, the additional value of the incurred debt is passed on through product purchase as wages for labour and rentals for capital. So the adventure capitalist gets a return on dollars invested and Labour has some income to purchase goods.

Again, another increase in real production cannot be paid for so more debt must be provided to absorb the increased product. This product must also be given over to the lender but cannot be for it has been consumed.

Because of the interest on the additional debt even more has been promised.

It cannot be paid for there is no real product to pay it off with. In money terms it is impossible to earn the money to purchase the incremental product.

Debt grows forever.

Since the promises to pay cannot be met, eventually the demand for product must be curtailed. The ability to pay is far outstripped by the need to pay.

Resources of debtors (secured collateral) are confiscated to repay lenders but lenders cannot lend or sell the assets to debt strapped borrowers. It may be tempting to sell the assets to wealthy foreigners as is happening today with wealthy Chinese citizens and the Chinese State buying assets across the developed world.

The economy winds down as the promised payments for past consumption cannot be paid. Money stops changing hands so frequently and then businesses and banks realise they have over-extended themselves, resulting in the normal credit-crunch, financial crisis and recession.

That was the theory which was set aside continuously so the correction to prices has yet to happen. Central planners kept doubling down with more debt. Amazing what the strong can do with the pure FIAT. The behavioural rules which govern FIAT currency were removed first under Reagan's watch and then completely under Clinton which caused intense inflation. This was because the rate of growth in supply of new money was in excess of additional value. M3 data tracks what the big boys are doing with their money which the FED stopped publishing in March, 2006.

Indeed, strange timing since in the first three months of 2006 M3 money supply went up an annualized 9.4%. A 9.4% increase in money supply should translate into a 9.4% inflation rate (if GDP produces exactly enough to counteract obsolescence). Even with a 1% increase in the supply of goods inflation would be 8.4%. The US government was reporting inflation to be 3.4% during this period.

An evil consequence was the off-shoring of tens of thousands of factories to China. The corporate executives had no choice, though they may not have understood their lack of choice at the System level—how many people can imagine the System in its totality? Since Central Bank and Federal Government action repeatedly halted market forces from clearing out ageing debt, the system continued to load extra debt onto corporate balance sheets so executives needed their rate of return to be higher than inflation just to be able to service their debts. If your rate of return is 2% but costs are inflating at 8.4% then there's no way to service your debts unless you find a way to cuts costs radically.

Government at all levels—local, state and federal—loved this arrangement as they could tax the inflation gains. The high inflation wiped away the present value of outstanding debt and aided in recycling old debt but also killed the US manufacturing and industrial base. US financial elites had by then realised a digital reserve currency allowed them to inflate the asset base of the entire Earth—the cost of usury began to compound at an exponential rate—though they failed to inform their "muppets" in Congress that China's Communist Party saw the exported factories and intellectual property as "collateral" for the trade debt.

The United States has been running trade debt in manufacturing for 4 decades straight, and in services for 3 decades. This was by Wall Street design because if competitive with trade surplus countries the dollar would have been too over valued to benefit the most parasitic sectors of the US economy, that is, the F.I.R.E. sectors: Finance; Insurance; Real Estate. For these non-value adding sectors trade debt was good as debt was required to maintain the appearance of actual GDP growth which stabilized their particular Ponzi while the country ran chronic current account deficits. The problem though is that any country that runs at a loss for too long is bankrupted which is the present situation for most of the West—the results of which shall visit American cities very soon.

Of course, endless war on evil, less dollar dependent countries was part of this agenda, a fact which became increasingly difficult to hide as a formerly dumb, contented public realized they were on the menu, too.

Since costs were inflating rapidly the only way for corporates to survive (service their debts) was to grow by cutting costs. Capitalism counts labour as a cost rather than as a potential asset and it's the largest cost in business, so it's the cost most rewarding to cut. Aided by Wall Street, executives exported manufacturing and cut their labour costs 75%-90%, but like every other instance of pulling demand forward or eating the seed corn, the law of diminishing returns means that once again they can't improve their balance sheets. Off-shoring was a one way ticket with one time benefits. So now executives are using every penny, including more debt, to buy back shares to rig earnings per share.

The problem is that for the profit to be realised the interest must be paid at some point or the bank would have to book a loss (and risk insolvency), so the bank needs to be covered by the issuance of new money to value that product at constant prices. That value has to be issued to somebody which will make everyone else jealous yet it must be done.

Debt jubilees do exactly that. Debt forgiveness issues retroactively the value of the money borrowed by each economic agent over the relevant period. If the agent borrowed a lot he receives the greatest issue of new money. If little then he receives little of the new money. Essentially the debtor is made whole for money promised and paid elsewhere.

Note that the problem exists even if the real product is not produced. **The act of purchase and payment of a money profit is a guarantee by the purchaser of the existence of incremental equivalent real value.** This may not be understood. If the real value does not exist by the standards of the general community this guarantee is fraudulent whether understood to be or not.

The consequence will be **inflation** as the value of transacting money will no longer be the same as the community's perception of real value. The purchase of anything is a guarantee that the value of the thing purchased meets a community standard however vaguely understood.

That's why the rate of interest must match growth in additional **value, not prices fixed by oligopolies. Adventure capitalists want a return on risk that's not being inflated away; and lenders should not be able to book inflated profits at their expense.**

Though eventually, the debt overhang must be repudiated or be cancelled with the free gift of an equivalent amount of money. Piecemeal repudiation as the economy slowly collapses is historically the most likely outcome through business failure. The alternative is the free issuance of money to purchase product which can be used by firms to pay down debt. Either way the debt is cancelled though the distribution of rewards is different.

It is not possible for a profit making, exchange economy with or without production to avoid this problem. It is built in and is not a question of socialism, capitalism or any other human ideology. Only a strictly zero profit economy can avoid it and a zero profit economy is a strictly no growth economy. It cannot even keep up with population growth. A socialist or Islamic economy that does not recognize profit is doomed to fail (which is why they usually fail).

New money must be issued as interest bearing debt to finance additional inputs and consumption. Or the equivalent in unpayable debt must be issued by mint or Central Bank. It amounts to the same thing in the end. The debt will either be repudiated or paid with new, freely issued money.

It will result in monetary collapse, slowly or quickly, if neither repudiated or issued new money as a gift. It is also why Capitalism as a force of modernity is largely absent in Islamic nations. Because Islam banned interest. Since 2008, we've seen piecemeal and staggered action by Central Banks to forgive unpayable debt.

Authorities claim to have assumed growth would return because historical data in the 1930s suggested it can, but that assumption is false due to terminal depletion of oil available to the real economy (not to mention the dying oceans). The recovery in the 30s was enabled by an increase in money supply AND net-energy gain from oil and gas.

Alas, our system framework was designed to accommodate growth and now it's negative; according to the Hills Group Report the World hit peak oil in 2012. How important is oil? The global economy consumes the energy of approximately 3 Cubic Miles of Oil annually from all sources—in 2006 oil provided 1.06, coal 0.81, natural gas 0.61, biomass 0.19, nuclear 0.15, hydroelectric 0.17. To replace oil, a 1GW nuclear or coal fired plant needs to be added every week for the next 50 years. Wind and solar will play their part but can't perform at that scale.

The system stress is unbearable; the corruption and misallocation enabled by the pure FIAT ensures the economy can't respond properly to the terminal depletion of oil; compare a few solar panels in California to China's plan to add 1 gigawatt of coal-fired capacity every week for the next four years.

Without growth in value there's no profit so the system is dead in the West. Money—commodities—more money required:

> But the stock of outstanding money in circulation will easily match the reduced output so no liquidity crisis or clamour for loans, check!
> Profit, thus defined, will trend toward zero, check!
> The banking sector will be profitless and shed jobs continuously and die a slow death, check!
> Interest rates go zero-bound as real output goes negative, check!
> Interest rates stay zero bound so marginal producers extract every drop of oil that's affordable for end-use consumers, check!
> Total value produced goes negative at constant prices—say -2% per year—but interest rates are stuck at the zero bound because folks will hold cash or Gold if authorities implement negative rates—so less income, declining standard of living for an increasing share of the populace, plus inflation! Check!

Now the lackeys for the bankers want to ban cash and enforce negative rates. Because according to economists that'll let them create infinite debt as pure investment; so no one will need savings any more. Even better, everyone will be indebted but the debt won't matter because the principal is automatically retired by negative rates. They'll dispense the debt (to their cronies) and give the sheep a minimum income. The banks then stay in business by taxing this minimum income as a fee for keeping the sheep's digital money safe.

Not a bad plan actually. If you're a really wise economist and really nice banker that can manage investments for 7.4 billion people it should work out really well (until you hear the automatic weapons fire.) The problem with the above framework—which is essentially the de facto framework—is that there's no mechanism to liquidate and free up the resources of companies producing less desirable goods. If a company is running at a loss it can simply access new debt, at zero cost, to recycle the ageing debt.

There's so much we can't measure any more. When you have a limitless system—infinite debt—there are no limits. Period. With "inflation" or the US Dollar long-term "devaluation" charts there's always some assumed underlying "true value" being measured against. It seems that "inflation" implies a closed system and a baseline marker. Not sure we have anything like that now: if one instrument has infinite potential then the entire system is infinite. We've essentially lost all ability to measure the economy—defined as a system that adds and delivers value to consumers.

Once an economy is **optimised** the following conditions are required for growth in **value** output:

1) Incremental increase in supply of interest bearing debt

2) Incremental increase in demand via imported bodies, or war, public works

3) Incremental increase in energy supply to the general economy

4) Incremental increase in inputs from the Natural System

Since there was no hope of domestic growth after peak oil in '74 the ideology known as Neo-Liberalism rose to pre-eminent power in the United States to justify the means required to prolong the original philosophy that had died—Growth in the wealth of the Dominant Class—which had to be done at the expense of democracy since the real economy was now a negative-sum game. Every evil imaginable has been brought to life:

➢ Plunder of Public Assets - privatize everything of value

➢ Intellectual Property - use oppressive patent law to prevent other suppliers from challenging your pricing

➢ Artificial Scarcity - buying up land and sitting on it (land banking) to restrict supply and keep prices high. Sitting on tons and tons of diamonds (De Beers) to restrict supply and fool people into thinking they're rare, hence maintaining high prices

➢ Economic Slavery - use slavery as a tool for political control (China)

➢ Destruction of Trade Unions and collective bargaining

- Free Trade - force domestic labour to compete with slave labour
- Debt Slavery - use debt rather than wages to finance consumption
- Import bodies to engage in low-productivity work as serving staff; this stimulates domestic demand and divides the population by lowering wages
- Push debt on weaker and corrupted nations and then plunder their Natural Resources e.g. Russia in the 90s
- And finally the Fiat, to tax the entire planet and destroy any that didn't pay

Our understanding progresses by accepting crises of economy are no longer natural. Before Capitalism crises occurred due to external factors such as war, disease and harvest failure. Now crises are created by the system. Now World War is required.

In a real economy being expanded by fossil fuels there was never enough money in circulation to grow real output which is essentially the story of Capital since 1709. Incremental growth in inputs was financed by issuing new money as debt bearing interest, so we can see a steady growth in promises owed though especially since the FIAT was unleashed. The industrialist bought the incremental increase in inputs with new debt but more money was required by consumers to absorb the added value.

And now we've run out of additional inputs so the System is finished.

What comes next? If you survive you may awake in the Dark Age. We've already tumbled back to the Middle Ages and if you listen closely you may hear St Aquinas say "I told you so."

You may experience a strong sensation of Déjà vu while reading about the Middle Age economy: it was a World where a small fraction of the population owned almost everything, where growth stagnated because of this and where long term interest rates went to zero for several hundred years because of this. It was a World without growth and little need for investment, thus the real opportunity cost of capital went to zero (in principle) leading to increased competition any place where equity still returned anything above zero. This meant margin erosion and return on equity eventually edging downwards towards zero. In the Middle Ages any asset that produced a reliable return (such as a central city property) had a price going to 'infinity' and a yield close to zero.

Sound familiar?

So what's the plan? Well that would depend upon whom you ask. The Chinese have achieved a near optimal setting for the present juncture:

1. Use **paper suppressed** Gold price to drive junior miners into bankruptcy or depressed stock price sale
2. Become the Worlds number one Gold producer
3. Develop a robust Shanghai Gold Exchange
4. Encourage and enable domestic population to save in Gold
5. Iran sanctions are lifted
6. Russia and satellite nations are supplying energy, inputs and high-technology
7. Good coal reserves and mature supply network
8. Develop a huge value adding economy
9. Integrate payment systems with strategic partners using domestic currencies
10. Integrate a Eurasian landmass economy which negates NATO's superior naval and aerial capabilities
11. Capture the manufacturing base of the West which acts as collateral for the trade debt

Essentially, the trade debt can't be repaid which alters the calculus for China going forward. What is the point in re-investing your surplus in the dollar economy when your return can never match the inflation rate? It's pointless to invest or hold dollars that are being debased rapidly, it's illogical to do so, and that's why the FED inflation figures are totally and completely baked. Why M3 isn't even published.

The only logical move in this environment is to go long; invest in Gold and wait for the monetary system to collapse. Because only Gold has the potential to exceed the rate of dollar inflation in the medium to long term. And survive the monetary collapse.

If investors figured this out; they would buy Gold and never sell it; just knuckle down and wait. If that behaviour spread; then the market would seize up. This is easy reasoning for those living in China for the Chinese state and banks advertise saving via Gold; and enable such with safe storage and purchase plans.

Though in the West things are entirely different. The Banking Capitalists are in power and treat those that undermine their privilege with violence and avarice. You do not buy Gold in abstract in the West, you buy it in a certain way, and all those ways create second- and third-order problems:

Where do I put it? Will it get taxed? Can I approach and sell it when I need it? Will it make me into a target in civil war? Will it reach my kids if something happens to me?

All sort of problems.

In what denominations? Ounces or official 11 kg pieces with numbers which stay in the system, but can be taken by the system or at least withheld from me ....

Tax problems - windfall gain taxes - normal taxation - wealth taxes?

If you're a real economy capitalist, and your company has a product with pricing power you can withstand bigger inflation. If you have not too much debt, the banks will not be able to steal your company in bad times. Monetary collapse is an abstract word—nobody knows how it will exactly play out—different factions have different agendas and different plans. It could bring on war or war could bring it on or most probably they will be interwoven and historians will lie about which caused which.

So Gold has a part to play in the West but not yet in the sphere of private investments. Nations which are being presently threatened with any kind of war by the "West"—Russia, China, Iran, Venezuela, Syria, etc.—they will all try not to hold Dollar reserves. They will switch to Roubles, Yuan, Gold, only maybe Euros, as anything could happen there.

We are in this process. If it accelerates a bull market psychology will erupt in metals and the Dollar will weaken. The New York banks know this, and this is the reason Dollar interest is higher (in March 2017, 1% on the short end, 2% on the 10 y) versus Europe or Japan. They actively try to magnet money back into the Dollar thereby counteracting official outflows (net trade deficit) and probably secret flows out of the Dollar.

"Hide your abilities and bide your time" was the advice left by Deng Xiaoping.

It appears perfect timing to forgive domestic debt and recapitalise the banks, the government and the population by letting Gold return to its historical value. Only Gold has the loyalty of elite and masses alike. And its unique properties can accommodate for deflation as demonstrated by its 6,000 year track record: the price of all goods being exchanged shall float to match the money derivatives (Bitcoin, banking credit, etc., of the Gold) in circulation. Only Gold and precious metals can deal with a shrinking system and redistribute wealth all at once.

The last gambit appears to have already been played: In January 2017, Chinese authorities began to enforce airtight capital controls which should remove external support for the numerous financial rackets wrapped around property in the West.

In the last analysis, Capitalism was a man-made system, designed to deliver Capital to the Dominant Class. The Banking Capitalists are the apex predators of the first universal Religion and have been in Political Power since the very beginning:

"The real truth of the matter is, as you and I both know, that a financial element in the large centers has owned the government ever since the days of Andrew Jackson."

President Roosevelt, in letter to banker representative Colonel House, November 21, 1933.

Unlike popular misconception, Capitalism is only about Capital, not about market economy or anything else. Markets existed before Capitalism, as well as monopoly. In the Gold Standard Era the risk of failure limited capital spending, but with removal of that natural anchor bankers allowed themselves to record profits in the present and kick the can—print more promises—if they didn't get paid. The circle of debt grew because the borrowers couldn't repay, since additional product, which may have been given over to lenders, was consumed instead. The surplus has been consumed so the interest can't be repaid—debt grows forever if not forgiven.

Historically, the unpayable debt disappears through business failure and with the advent of FIAT—inflation. Capitalists plugged into the State and Military Industrial Complex had the pricing power to withstand the inflation, though investors in the consumer economy required the rate of return to be higher than inflation so the economy that actually served the population was slowly and eventually starved of investment.

The end of easy oil meant peak output and affordability for the USA, and Neo-Liberalism introduced a lot of destructive policies to continue the flow of capital to the Dominant Class. The FIAT placed a tax on the entire planet which financed war, robbery and Empire.

The energy sectors supply to the real economy shrinks so quality of goods delivered to the US of C is forced lower as affordability declines. An increasing fraction of humans are without income earning opportunity so revolt by peasants and mass death beckons. The function of the petrodollar begins to wane with depleting oil so foreign currencies and economies are targeted for destruction—creating fresh demand for newly printed Dollars—though Gold is the ultimate outcome as the competing system is unfazed.

FIAT inflation seizes evermore buying power from agents in the Real Economy causing assets to flow to the top so no more growth is possible since the rate of return approaches zero while the price of assets goes toward infinity; therefore the system ends and the medieval style of economy returns. What next? Death, and then...

The Dark Age.

The Key to Defeat America

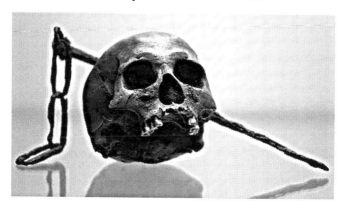

There is more to the Russian and Chinese psyche than statistics, or the projected impressions of outsiders can comprehend.

Ethnicity is forged in the furnace of experience. And unlike some "ancient" peoples, the Chinese are not only one of the oldest and most complex cultures, but, more importantly, they have a living and continuous memory, something that to take other "ancient" peoples by comparison, escapes the modern Egyptians entirely and the Greeks to a very great extent.

American "ethnicity," young and vibrant, is still being forged. It is strong but brittle by comparison. For all its power, it could very well break if struck against that massive wall of "ethnic tribalism."

That right there is the key to defeat America.

In his seminal book, Benedict Anderson points out that all national communities are "imagined." However, there are a handful that includes China, and Russia to a different capacity, whose sense of ethnicity is a powerful factor in their collective performance that makes statistical analysis both incomplete and distorting.

JFK hired "the best and the brightest" that the modern age had to offer to form his cabinet and fight the Vietnam war. Robert McNamara and others were ready to explode the myth-based world of South-East Asia with the irresistible force of technology, statistics and body counts. But the incalculable, and to the Americans unfathomable, "élan" of Vietnamese ethnicity—

deeply imagined and more powerful than any contemporary "reality"—produced one of the most stunning military defeats in human history.

So America has been beaten before and can be beaten again. To understand how, the Russians need to comprehend the ambition and greed of our Dominant Class—its factions and mechanics—and please appreciate reader, that the mode of cognition by our noble families is shaped more by classical language than any other. Theirs is a story of struggle and supremacy throughout the Ages—from humble merchant to Dominant Position—adapting by deception is their preferred modus operandi.

Their primary concern was always protecting the Religion which prolongs their Dominance. Capitalism requires expansion which means the logical result is World-wide Conquest, and subjugation of all Races.

A Universal Fascist State arising from and shaped by *Confidence, Power and Empire*.

Confidence that one would get one's Gold for dollars—broken first for US citizen by Roosevelt in 1933 and for nations by Nixon in 1971. Cutting this link to Gold was cutting the external anchor impeding war and deficit spending. The promise of Gold for dollars was revoked, **one** could only exchange a dollar for two times 50 cents from that moment on. A non-US-central bank could still buy Gold on the open market, but it presumably would not come out of US Gold reserves and soon cost much more. Also, it would expose itself in not playing along with international central bank politics decided upon by The Powers That Be.

Now even the "old gold" from the '50s and '60s trade surpluses are not handed out to Germany.

One can still buy Gold in different forms and quantities and locations, so there is still a connection between the two and though no one would call it a "gold-anchored dollar", to some extent it still is. The price of Gold in dollars (or dollars in Gold) still matters psychologically, confirming or undermining confidence in the current FIAT system. Though one can see confidence like sand running out, the hourglass waiting to be turned.

Next is Power.

The Power to define the rules, 1944 in Bretton Woods, against the British then; to draw the reserve currency privilege from bankrupt Britain to the sole new world power, the USA.

Power to keep the Gold **physically** in New York—tested first by De Gaulle around 1966. He sent a destroyer to get France's Gold home. On board it may have taken ill with something we now call "color revolution." The Empire's virus—released in 1953, Persia—broke out on the streets of Paris in 1968 and, not much later, De Gaulle was on pension and George Pompidou moved from Banque Rothschild to Palace Elysée.

The US had the power to **effectively** redefine "reserves" and they used it: Up to 1971 "reserves" of foreign central banks were mostly Gold reserves at the Fed in New York. From then on any additional reserves would primarily be US government bonds held at the Fed. These reserves would be acquired by US trade deficits in the old-fashioned way but also could be mutually created *ex-nihilo* out of Swap lines between central banks or from Special Drawing Rights *by* the IMF.

Now some central banks and Sovereign wealth funds (Japan, Israel, Norway, Switzerland, etc.) have moved reserves **from government bonds** even into equities. One of the pioneers of this, Stanley Fisher as former head of the Israeli Central bank, now sits prominently on the Fed's board.

And then Empire.

Imperial infrastructure only grew with time as additional inputs were required.

An important source of inputs was the systematically depopulated island of Ireland. Ireland is a fertile landmass capable of producing a super abundance of foodstuffs, but a continuous surplus is only possible with a policy of low population density. Systematic depopulation of Ireland from the mid-nineteenth century began when a blight infected the staple food of the native population and the British Government continued to allow the export of alternative nutrition—grain and protein sources—to the British Island.

Nassau Senior, an economics professor at Oxford University, wrote that the Famine "would not kill more than one million people, and that would scarcely be enough to do any good." In 1848, Denis Shine Lawlor suggested that English Premier Russell was a student of the Elizabethan poet Edmund Spenser, who had calculated "how far English colonisation and English policy might be most effectively carried out by Irish starvation." Charles Trevelyan, the civil servant with most direct responsibility for the government's handling of the famine, described it in 1848 as "a direct stroke of an all-wise and all-merciful Providence", which laid bare "the deep and inveterate root of social evil"; he affirmed that the Famine was "the sharp but effectual remedy by which the cure is likely to be effected. God grant that the generation to which this opportunity has been offered may rightly perform its part…"

The 1841 census of Ireland showed a population of just over eight million. By 1911 this had halved to four million. By 1960 the population of the Irish Republic was 2.9 million—A people diminished to the role of producing a **secure** supply of food to the heart of Empire. Depopulation can be achieved by breaking **faith** in the nation via induced famine, starvation, state sponsored terrorism, financial and monetary attacks, war, civil war and economic war. **Belief** can be broken by **corruption of moral standards**. Ireland's ever growing surplus of food powered Imperial armies on a World-wide march.

The Suez Canal Company came into being on the 15th of December 1858, and over the next 11 years the canal was built. And although the British recognised the canal as an important trade route they objected to the use of forced Egyptian labour to build it, and perceived the French project as a threat to their geopolitical and financial interests.

Initially, international opinion was sceptical and Suez Canal Company shares did not sell well overseas. Britain, the United States, Austria and Russia did not buy any shares, although all French shares were quickly sold in France. The canal opened to shipping on the 17th of November 1869, and had an immediate and dramatic effect on world trade, playing an important role in increasing European penetration and colonization of Africa.

External debts forced Said Pasha's successor, Isma'il Pasha, to put up Egypt's shares for sale. In 1875, the London banking house of N M Rothschild &

Sons advanced the Prime Minister, Benjamin Disraeli, acting for the British Government, the vast sum of £4,000,000 to purchase Suez Canal shares.

Disraeli was a close personal friend of Lionel de Rothschild, and according to legend, this was transacted on a gentleman's agreement, with no documentation, a technically unsecured loan for a sum of over £550 million today. The legend has it that when Baron de Rothschild enquired "What is your security?" the reply was "The British government." The Baron ate some grapes, spat out the pips, and declared "Done."

Disraeli and ally, her Majesty Queen Victoria, were motivated by lust for power to strengthen dominance over her Majesty's colony—India. After her victory of securing ownership of the Suez Canal she was awarded the title Empress of India. (And reader, please note that Egypt's premier had become compromised by external debts.)

Another important building block of Empire was set up by Prime Minister David Lloyd George for British Big Oil circa 1917, with the divide and conquest of local tribes by the Sykes–Picot Agreement. And no one, today, ever seems to notice that Israel is a narrow, strategic land bridge that splits the Islamic world in two—separating North Africa and Egypt from South-west Asia—and also protects the Suez Canal.

Lloyd George saw the value but a long term military occupation would have been ruinously expensive. So he looked around for a people dumb enough to take on the job for free and issued the Balfour Declaration. As James Renton notes in "The Zionist Masquerade", **British intelligence covertly took over the small Zionist movement.**

In 1973 geopolitics was brought into pre-eminent play by the OPEC embargo after the Yom-Kippur war. Back in World War II, FDR and the Office of Strategic Services (now known as the CIA) had set up Arabia and Persia as a geopolitical protectorate of the USA with Britain now as a junior partner, handing the oil areas to a few sheikhs and a shah, performed according to the usual divide-et-impera manual.

So the 'petrodollar' did not start with Kissinger. The Nobel Peacemaker only activated it by "allowing" the Arabs to cartelize oil, milking US consumers and the surplus economies of Europe and Japan, recycling petrodollars into US and Israeli weapons, wars and dollar deposits at international banks, thus greatly expanding the Eurodollar market.

Saudi Arabia, the Gulf Sheikdoms and Persia—they were all added to the new dollar zone, guaranteed by half a dozen floating aircraft carriers, a landed one in Palestine and the CIA everywhere. And by the way, Big-Oil became a politically and strategically important instrument. So the dollar from then was backed by 'black gold' and as Professor Krugman admitted in an irritated interview "men with guns".

In the late 90s, with GATT and most favored nation status for China the game continued with China and Emerging Markets constructing their monetary systems upon dollars earned or borrowed, building up infrastructure and export economies, again providing dollar reserves in a virtuous loop. **The Yuan-fix to the dollar (after a devaluation) in the mid-1990s put China into the dollar-zone.** But now geopolitics has switched radically. Hard to say when though historians may point to Putin's speech at the Munich Security Conference in 2007 or the beginning of his second presidency in 2011, or possibly with the Russian-Chinese trade and defense pacts in 2014—where they seem to have bound their destinies together—against the Empire.

Anyway, we now know the game has definitely changed. The Reserve Currency role of the dollar is in question—as John Kerry admitted recently before camera. For some years now some countries are trying to get away from the dollar slowly while the US tries to collapse their financial systems. In a paradoxical and hard-to-grasp way a simultaneous run into and out of the dollar has begun: Russia and Brazil are best examples of what happens to you if you do not have enough reserves of a reserve currency you actually do not want to hold—but have to, because your monetary system is built upon it.

Too much reserves and best case its value gets slowly or less slowly inflated away (with zero or maybe soon negative interest as compensation), worst case frozen by a US enemy act or decree (see Iran early 80s); not enough of them and your *local* currency comes under attack by the banks and hedge funds looking to short it into a hole provoking and causing (or being provoked and being caused by) capital flight and color revolution. Nobody knows what the right amount of dollar reserves should be under these circumstances, or more to the point, if such a right amount even exists.

Such enemy action is justified by ancient insight. Reader, please recall the Melian Dialogue:

[Athenians.] "For ourselves, we shall not trouble you with specious pretences - either of how we have a right to our empire because we overthrew the Mede, or are now attacking you because of wrong that you have done us - and make a long speech which would not be believed; and in return we hope that you, instead of thinking to influence us by saying that you did not join the Lacedaemonians, although their colonists, or that you have done us no wrong, will aim at what is feasible, holding in view the real sentiments of us both; since you know as well as we do that Right, as the world goes, is only in question between equals in power, while the strong do what they can and the weak suffer what they must."

The critical line is the last one, **"The strong do what they can and the weak suffer what they must."** There is no more concise analysis of contemporary events and the core of American foreign policy. I suppose "Fuck the EU" was a more concise version of same.

The removal of classical history and literature from the general curriculum in the West recognised that the masses no longer had to be educated, but were to be "trained", instead. People think they are well-informed if they read the newspapers—that they know what is really going on. Amazing, really. Sheep grazing in a meadow are less complacent.

What is in bankrupt Ukraine that justifies provoking even a limited nuclear conflict that could kill billions from crop failure alone? Nothing.

But the Empire will do everything to keep the monetary charade alive—for it must, for that is how it's financed—including all sorts and forms of war: sanctions, blockades, assassinations, color revolutions, hacking war, kinetic war, orbital war and maybe even nuclear war.

And the Empire doesn't do accidental war, what you are witnessing today are the plays of very deep games:

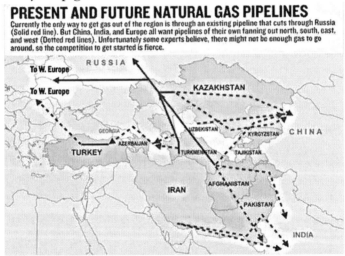

1) Washington is not in Afghanistan out of charity—we are there because Afghanistan is the lynch-pin of the Empire's plan to loot Central Asia and conquer the entire Earth.

2) Afghanistan is key to Washington's plan to screw Iran out of the revenue from selling gas to Pakistan and India by having Exxon and Chevron transport gas from Turkmenistan instead. See the TAPI Pipeline (Turkmenistan-Afghanistan-Pakistan-India.) It will feed China eventually as well.

3) Afghanistan is also key to Washington's plan to displace Russia from supplying 35% of the EU's gas input—by running a pipeline from Turkmenistan under the Caspian Sea to Azerbaijan and from there along Chevron's existing Baku-Tbilisi-Ceyhan oil pipeline to Turkey. Washington has been pushing the Transcaspian Gas Pipeline since the 1990s. And when the subversion/conquest of Ukraine is complete, we can simply plug the Transcaspian Gas Pipeline into the existing Ukrainian distribution network that already feeds the EU.

4) It is not just the money, although Exxon and Chevron have invested around $50 billion in the Caspian in the past two decades. If we also control the EU's gas supply as well as her oil supplies from the Middle East—all priced in Dollars—then we control the 17 Trillion $ GDP of the EU. Well, more than we already do. The CIA controls Europe politically—control files and such—note the immediate agreement by all official heads of state to invite Ukraine into the EU economy after the coup in Kiev, and blanket support by the official media.

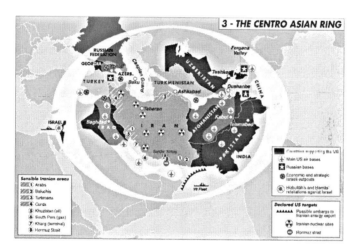

5) Afghanistan is next door to Turkmenistan and the Caspian—and our bases there are key to military protection of Big Oil's massive investments in looting Central Asia.

6) The idea that the nine bases are temporary leases until the Taliban is beaten is hilarious. The lease says: "It [the lease] shall remain in force until the end of 2024 AND BEYOND, unless terminated pursuant to paragraph 4 of this Article."[two year advance notice]. We "leased" Guantanamo Bay from Cuba in

1934, which is an excellent lesson on how these things turn out.

7) Moscow and several Russian nuclear ICBM sites will be within range of our RQ-180 broadband stealth drones (carrying the 300 kiloton B61 nuclear warhead) when they are based in Ukraine—that is why Washington was also strongly pushing for Ukraine to be admitted into NATO back in 2008 over the strong protests of France and Germany.

However, there are two Russian ICBM sites in central Russia that are out of range of Ukraine but within range of Afghanistan. If we take out Russia's nuclear forces in a First Strike—and threaten to shut off China's oil with a US Navy embargo—then our Oligarchs will finally have conquered the entire Earth.

And it is slightly ironic, but our RQ-180 stealth drone is the perfect suicide bomber—Range of 1200 miles, untraceable as to origin and capable of carrying a 300 Kt nuke. And why would we use a stealth drone to deliver a nuclear bomb? The answer is that if you deliver it via an ICBM, the missile's radar track tells the enemy you are the attacker and you should receive his retaliation. The whole idea of deterrence via Mutually Assured Destruction can now be doubted.

How would Russia know the source of the attack if it is delivered by an invisible stealth drone? Would the survivors want to fight a disastrous nuclear war with an innocent USA—and suffer the consequence of ethnic extinction—if China might be the attacker? Such a First Strike would be a bolt out of the blue with synchronised delivery of payload.

There is also Britain's Taranis stealth drone as possible delivery system. Stated take-off weight for the Taranis is 18,000 lbs, the weight of a 300 kt B61 nuclear bomb is only 700 lbs so she may be able to carry multiple nukes in her weapons bay.

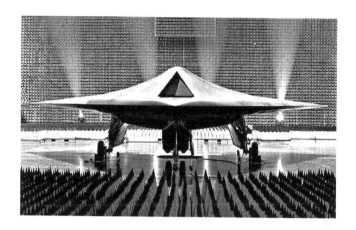

From photos, Taranis appears to have a "broadband stealth" design – i.e, capable of deflecting radars of multiple frequencies and hence invisible even to Russian and Chinese advanced radars. If you are not carrying a human pilot, you don't need to return and that doubles range. The advertised range of the US Global Hawk is 1400 miles and the Taranis may be able to match that if kept at higher altitudes where the air is thin. Regarding her range, the program coyly states "intercontinental".

If applied against fixed targets, the autonomous guidance system of Taranis (or RQ-180) can be programmed to attack multiple locations using GPS, without the need for a high bandwidth video comm link to a human operator. With such a link, she could hunt, track and attack mobile targets like Russia's mobile ICBMs. Or "I can build a platform and I can give it autonomous capability, and tell it 'go into this area and kill anything that moves,'" said Gen Mike Hostage, commander of Air Combat Command in 2012.

Long distance laser communications in the distortion-free vacuum of space have already been demonstrated. NASA's recent successes with such technology will allow construction of military communications relays with far higher bandwidth than what is available today using microwave. It removes a technical risk from certain architectures.

Architectures that will allow Washington to conquer all of Earth.

And one should clarify: China might be the attacker if she was trying to provoke a major war between Russia and USA/UK (in a time of tension such as now) so that China would be the last hegemon standing. That would be the Franklin Roosevelt strategy—please compare Russian and German casualties in WWII with those of the US in the European theatre.

Washington's promotion of the Transcaspian Pipeline from Turkmenistan to Turkey (and now to Ukraine) was a direct threat to Russia's South Stream and to Russia's economy. An alternative pipeline to the EU would go through Syria which is the policy motive behind the vicious war there.

A merciless mercantile policy with all the "international collaboration" of a python squeezing a baby pig to death. You see, these are long games being played, blowing up an enemy's factories with bombs is costly. Far easier to first reduce him to nothing by undercutting him in commercial competition to ensure the factories go bankrupt. Then attack him later when he has been weakened. Same duelling principle as slicing an artery and then waiting. And it's not just the US, Germany has also disrobed her enemies.

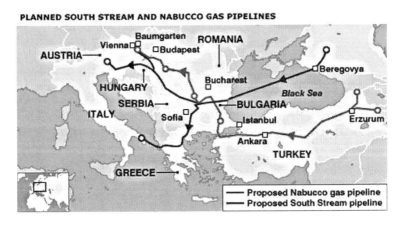

This is a fight to the death for Russia. And she's losing. Putin's problem is that Russia is a nation of chess players who never learned American poker. Chess begins as a game between equals so why has Putin played chess? Buying time can strengthen Russia somewhat but ultimately US 2012 GDP was $16.2 Trillion, Russia's only $2 Trillion. So in a bidding war for Ukraine's oligarchs, Russia will lose.

But the crafty Chinese knew 2500 years ago that an enemy's greatest weakness lies at the base of his strength (Lao Tzu). If Putin rattles the china a little, our Oligarchs have far more to lose than Russia.

For example, Putin could evacuate Russia's cities—the opening kick-off to a nuclear exchange under Cold War rules (and are there any other kind?) It takes 3 days to evacuate US cities (around 5 for New York) and so the Pentagon would be forced to respond, even if they are sure Putin is bluffing.

That would rock Wall Street and The City, sink the stock market and trigger the next leg of the Depression. After a week or so, Putin could start moving his people back. Wait for the US to do the same and then three weeks later, do the same thing again. Nothing that justifies a military attack by the USA but one which staggers US financial systems repeatedly. Hurts Russia's economy as well but who loses the most?

Such adds an element of understanding of Russia's testing of nuclear bunkers in the Summer of 2016—a warning from Putin that he was preparing to play poker. And Russian "ethnicity" protected him from dissent or revolution. Can the same be said of the United Kingdom or the USA? Was the psyche of African Americans wrought within the same furnace of experience as Anglo-Saxon Americans? What of the mental life of Native, Mexican or Irish Americans? Are there more shared experiences than different?

Any ethnic group is always struggling to balance the forces of inclusion and exclusion. You can see the extremes of inclusion trying to encompass the entire world: with NGO's "helping" backward and tribal populations cross the carrying capacity of their locality. With bureaucrats in Brussels trying to foster the concept of a pan-European ethnicity via media instruments such as Euro News. Such attempts are doomed to fail as the forces of exclusion are empowered by energy and resource scarcity.

The referendum for Scottish Independence provides an illuminating example of such forces at work. Inclusive Scots voted to remain a part of England and so the referendum failed to pass by a tiny margin. Now that English citizens have voted for Brexit and exclusivity; those inclusive Scots that voted against independence shall feel betrayed and project their fantasy of inclusion toward a pan-European identity. The First Minister of Scotland is already preparing the ground for a second referenda that shall surely pass.

Great caution is required (especially before attracting the attention of Imperial Instruments.) There is a difference between *de jure* and *de facto* sovereignty—and it was the recognition of that difference that caused the UK and Ireland to join the EEC—and Ireland to remain in the EU. Firstly, a capitalistic nation can only enjoy unfettered de facto sovereignty if it can sustain a self-contained complex economy—autarky.

De jure sovereignty is a state of affairs that is in accordance with law though has no value if it cannot in fact be exercised e.g. present day Ukraine. The EU is a massive *de jure* sovereignty pool, which had the effect of enhancing its member states *de facto* sovereignty, albeit by acting collectively. It would be foolish to throw away much of your *de facto* sovereignty to pursue the chimera of independence.

But England's elite started the class war, by taxing producers rather than the hoarders of land, by importing terrorists and other undesirable burdens to inflate the financial racket wrapped around property, and so they lack the moral authority to navigate these treacherous waters.

Putin also understands the Greek "crisis" was contrived to provoke European fiscal integration. It is only with European debt, i.e. Portuguese debt backed by the Germans (and conversely), that the European state could be considered to exist (and would become extremely difficult to dissolve). Similarly the modern US superstate would not exist had Hamilton not done to US states what the elites are planning for EU countries.

The attack on Deutsche Bank as well as the Greek Crisis was meant for that same principal goal to be achieved: EU fiscal integration and the building of an EU superstate. Russia doesn't desire such as that superstate would be a US vassal and artificially isolated from Russia. **The EU's huge value added economy would then appear to back the US Dollar, and appearances are important as they influence *faith* and recognition of hegemony.** It would also greatly prevent Eurasian collaboration, and would render impossible a strong Berlin-Moscow-Beijing axis.

It is difficult, if not impossible, for an alien culture or sub-group to take advantage, subvert, or destroy a nation when the host culture is homogenous, certain, confident and content. What we call western media is nothing less than a battering ram used to break down cultural norms and barriers in order to subvert each and every western nation into submission. You are at war whether you like it or not—with a parasitic culture that is hell-bent on destruction—and that culture requires Globalism for its continuing power and survival. The fact that it is socially unacceptable to even discuss these matters shows just how powerful the parasite has become.

Yuri Bezemnov (Soviet spy defector, 1984): "The demoralization process in the United States is basically completed already for the last 25 years. Actually, it's over fulfilled because demoralization now reaches such areas where not even Comrade Andropov and all his experts would even dream of such tremendous success. Most of it is done by Americans to Americans thanks to lack of moral standards. As I mentioned before, exposure to true information does not matter anymore. A person who was demoralized is unable to assess true information. The facts tell nothing to him, even if I shower him with information, with authentic proof, with documents and pictures ... he will refuse to believe it ... That's the tragedy of the situation of demoralization.

The next stage is destabilization.... It only takes 2 to 5 years to destabilize a nation. This time what matters is essentials; economy, foreign relations, [and] defense systems. And you can see it quite clearly that in some... sensitive areas such as defense and [the] economy, the influence of Marxist-Leninist ideas in the United States is absolutely fantastic. I could never believe it 14 years ago when I landed in this part of the world that the process will go that fast.

Most of the American politicians, media, and educational system train another generation of people who think they are living at the peacetime. False. United States is in a state of war; undeclared, total war against the basic principles and foundations of this system. And the initiator of this war is not Comrade Andropov of course—it's the system. However, ridiculous it may sound, [it is] the world Communist system, or the world Communist conspiracy. Whether I scare some people or not, I don't give a hoot. If you're not scared by now, nothing can scare you."

And after our Oligarchs have completed their conquest of Russia, we will all be slaves.

One of the problems of Capitalism is labour redundancy—and the genius of our Dominant Class is that they made Demoralising the redundant profitable—far better than repressing or killing them. The goal of demoralistion is that they don't value anything; so they'll accept anything.

The media have a lot to answer for. It's not the "mainstream media". That train left the station during the 2008 season of 'Change We Can Believe In'. Can you recollect when Obama, McCain and Bush all got together for a press conference during the Obama vs. McCain election to tell the American public that the bank bailouts were a good thing and were going to happen, thereby temporarily removing any doubt about who they all worked for. Call it what it is: State Media. State TV. State-Run News Agencies. The genius of mainstream media is that Americans actually pay to get brainwashed. Yeah, that's right, state news is not free in America, the Retards actually pay for Fox News. That's amazing. What an achievement—our Oligarchs made brainwashing profitable.

John Swinton, Chief editorial writer of the New York Times from 1860-70:

"There is no such thing as a free press. You know it and I know it. There is not one of you who would dare to write his honest opinions. The business of the journalist is to destroy truth, to lie outright, to pervert, to vilify, to fawn at the feet of Mammon, and to sell himself, his country, and his race, for his daily bread. We are tools and vassals of rich men behind the scenes. We are jumping jacks; they pull the strings, we dance; our talents, our possibilities, and our lives are the property of these men. We are intellectual prostitutes."

The Communist manual of instructions in psychological warfare stated:

'The first thing to degrade in any nation is the state of man himself. Nations which have a high ethical tone are difficult to conquer. Their loyalties are hard to break, their allegiances are fanatical, and what they usually call their spiritual integrity cannot be violated by duress. Man must be degraded from a spiritual being to an animalistic pattern. He must think of himself as an animal...

According to Yuri Bezemnov the system was called Subversion:

That is subvert anything of value in the target country, until perception of reality is so screwed up that he does not see you as an enemy. He noted that no one could subvert Japan because Japan was a closed country, pre-WW2. The media are "unelected … Who are they? Why are they not elected? They're a bunch of enfeebled snobs." (See Volume 1+2) How do you know they're not intelligence placements, either foreign or domestic?

A special example is Dick Cheney secretly using reporter Judith Miller to plant a story—about Saddam Hussein making nukes with aluminum tubes—on the front page of the New York Times and then going on US TV networks the next day and citing the same story as justification for his argument that Saddam was trying to build nukes.

One should use bureaucrats to weaken communal ties and connectivity. Social workers only want a pay-check; they're not motivated by spiritual feeling or moral obligation: "A cop is a pig…he abuses his power…a criminal is cool, oppressed and creative."

"No religion mentions equality, just the opposite … by your deeds you'll be judged." People are equal—everyone's above average—that's a lie, a deliberate foundation of sand so you'll collapse.

Equal opportunities—why? To excel? No. It's because equality can then be super-imposed from above, from bureaucracy. When there's no right or wrong nothing works anymore. Constructive compromise becomes impossible between citizens—traditional norms of behaviour are destabilised—labour relations are radicalised, e.g. the more heroic protesters they appear the better—violence is considered normal, common-place—militarisation of the populace is encouraged.

Now court cases decide everything, the society becomes antagonistic, the media is in opposition to society, alienated from society—e.g. a homosexual was politically asleep for 20 years, now it's a political issue, he's dividing the populace e.g. gay marriage—the goal of destabilisation period is antagonistic clash.

Hostile actors' spring into the vacuum of power—they use force if necessary —unelected committees or bureaucrats exercise state powers (See Southern Europe during debt crisis, Greece, ECB, FED, democratically elected Berlusconi replaced by "technical government" led by banker Mario Monti, etc.)

The population wants a saviour (Obama) ... dictator (Erdogan)... strong man (el-Sisi), population is sick and tired—there are now two options: Civil war Lebanon style or invasion Afghanistan style (with outside leadership flown in.)

The next phase is Normalisation—idealists that championed their cause are executed or silenced—for the foreign leadership need stability to exploit the nation, to seize resources and take advantage of the victory. (See Ireland 2008 onwards.) Stop importation of ideas that are alien to traditional morality and Religion is the best way to stop all subversion. Civilizational Disintegration begins when the traditional Religion which holds society together disintegrates. (See Volume 1 and lectures by Bezemnov.)

The goal of the unofficial elite is to control "all habitable space on the planet," the ultimate play is securing all resources so no rival power can emerge. You may use the word Globalism or Absolutism to describe their ideology but the result is the same. What are they capable of? Everything and anything that they can do.

Please study how things evolved with the conquest of Transvaal Gold mines in 1900 and the instrument of victory—the first known usage of concentration camps. Look below to see what that looked like:

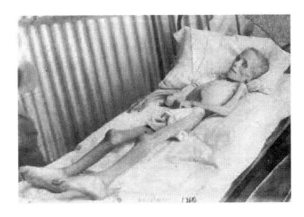

We even have it in writing.

The Wolfowitz Doctrine announces the U.S's status as the world's only remaining superpower following the collapse of the Soviet Union at the end of the Cold War and proclaims its main objective to be retaining that status.

> Our first objective is to prevent the re-emergence of a new rival, either on the territory of the former Soviet Union or elsewhere, that poses a threat on the order of that posed formerly by the Soviet Union. This is a dominant consideration underlying the new regional defense strategy and requires that we endeavor to prevent any hostile power from dominating a region whose resources would, under consolidated control, be sufficient to generate global power.

The doctrine establishes the U.S.'s leadership role within the new world order.

> The U.S. must show the leadership necessary to establish and protect a new order that holds the promise of convincing potential competitors that they need not aspire to a greater role or pursue a more aggressive posture to protect their legitimate interests. In non-defense areas, we must account sufficiently for the interests of the advanced industrial nations to discourage them from challenging our leadership or seeking to overturn the established political and economic order. We must maintain **the mechanism** for deterring potential competitors from even aspiring to a larger regional or global role.

The doctrine downplays the value of international coalitions.

> Like the coalition that opposed Iraqi aggression, we should expect future coalitions to be ad hoc assemblies, often not lasting beyond the crisis being confronted, and in many cases carrying only general agreement over the objectives to be accomplished. Nevertheless, the sense that the world order is ultimately backed by the U.S. will be an important stabilizing factor.

The doctrine stated the U.S's right to intervene when and where it believed necessary.

> While the U.S. cannot become the world's policeman, by assuming responsibility for righting every wrong, we will retain the preeminent responsibility for addressing selectively those wrongs which threaten not only our interests, but those of our allies or friends, or which could seriously unsettle international relations.

The doctrine highlighted the possible threat posed by a resurgent Russia.

> We continue to recognize that collectively the conventional forces of the states formerly comprising the Soviet Union retain the most military potential in all of Eurasia; and we do not dismiss the risks to stability in Europe from a nationalist backlash in Russia or efforts to reincorporate into Russia the newly independent republics of Ukraine, Belarus, and possibly others... We must, however, be mindful that democratic change in Russia is not irreversible, and that despite its current travails, Russia will remain the strongest military power in Eurasia and the only power in the world with the capability of destroying the United States.

The doctrine clarified the overall objectives in the Middle East and Southwest Asia.

> In the Middle East and Southwest Asia, our overall objective is to remain the predominant outside power in the region and preserve U.S. and Western access to the region's oil. We also seek to deter further aggression in the region, foster regional stability, protect U.S. nationals and property, and safeguard our access to international air and seaways. As demonstrated by Iraq's invasion of Kuwait, it remains fundamentally important to prevent a hegemon or alignment of powers from dominating the region. This pertains especially to the Arabian peninsula. Therefore, we

must continue to play a role through enhanced deterrence and improved cooperative security.

Call it what you will ... Absolutism ... Globalism or a New World Order; it was always a psychotic fantasy enabled by the historically unique conditions created by oil discovery.

A fantasy presently being wrecked on the shoals of resource depletion, exclusive Tribalism, and the fact that the mind forms differently in different places: specially important are the psycho-spatial forces within nation states and trading blocs. For instance, those who live in densely populated areas need a political economy that is routinely responsive, highly coordinated, systematized and has support and redundant systems in situ. In contrast, rural dwellers subjected to the cost and static nature of the same political economy would chafe and complain bitterly of a loss of liberty.

For example, the people who inhabit Tibet resent a political economy that was designed to address the needs of densely populated Eastern China. Within the federated continental economy of the United States, sparsely populated states vote 'Red' while densely populated states vote 'Blue'.

Or contemplate how the constantly shifting landscape of sand dunes in the Arabian peninsula leaves the locals hostile to iconography and idols that promise a sense of certainty. For them, impermanence is part of God's design. In the face of such complexity and variability, those who continue to advance a global government would seem to be dreaming.

Furthermore, a major mental difference between the New World and Old World is that there is a deeper appreciation of history in Eurasia. The US Congressional Report explains what caused the bankruptcy of the Russian People in 1998:

"The road to this crisis had been littered with warning signs that the Clinton administration ignored for years. The U.S. encouragement of increasingly massive loans to the Russian central government from the IMF continued despite the lack of basic free market legislation in place to justify it. With no market in banking services, no reliable protection for private property rights, no mortgage lending, and no commercial dispute resolution, capital flight—

fueled by IMF hard currency—approached 10% of Russia's gross domestic product."

[Translation: Clinton loaned money to Russia, turned a blind eye to Russian politicians stealing the loan money and sending it to their Swiss bank accounts, and thereby putting the Russian people into debt slavery. See also Argentina.]

The Report continues:

"In early August 1998, President Clinton was concerned about his scheduled September 1998 summit with Yeltsin." The White House dispatched a Treasury Department official to Moscow "to ensure that the show stays on the road for the next three weeks at least."

On Monday, August 17, the Russian government formally declared its insolvency, and horrific economic consequences followed rapidly. The Clinton troika strategy of massive lending to the central government as a substitute for the construction of a free enterprise system in Russia had proved an error of historic proportions.

The administration had, in effect, hijacked the IMF to implement its economic strategy, and the IMF debt, far from solving Russia's problems, had exacerbated its difficulties. But despite having engineered the entire series of loans that contributed to Russia's complete economic collapse, the Clinton administration immediately attempted to distance itself from the fiasco.

"It was the Russians' choice," said one Clinton administration official.

Few in Russia accepted this version of events. Many Russians, not surprisingly, blamed the West, the IMF, and the United States for intentionally leading Russia down the path of ruin. The heavy-handed and wrong-headed involvement of Clinton administration officials in Russian government economic policy made America an easy scapegoat for disgruntled Russians.

"Since the beginning of the Clinton administration, U.S. officials had urged a steady diet of borrowing to mask the Russian economy's fundamental weaknesses prolonging and deepening the eventual collapse."

Amazing how the historical record appears to chime in perfectly with the Wolfowitz Doctrine. Almost like someone had a plan.

So Putin can wait for NATO to install stealth bombers and nukes in Ukraine —the drone base is already operational in Afghanistan. At which point, Russia will have the choice of launching the ICBMs to destroy America or face eternal enslavement. Or Putin could play poker with The Families. They would then answer the only existential question in economics: What's the present value of the Dollar if there's a real risk that Washington won't exist next week?

The wealth of our Oligarchs is predicated upon our Imperial Instruments. But the continuing power of our Imperial Instruments is decided by The Families—for our Empire is financed by the FIAT—and guess who the senior bondholders are? Our noble families have a deep understanding of Empire for Imperialism preceded Capitalism. Throughout the Ages, they have adapted, often by deception, and used the darkest of the dark arts to bring down Kings and Generals—to make a would be Empress come cap in hand —for the hand that gives is above the hand that takes. You cannot imagine the vicious and evil power struggles which allowed Capitalism to find its own footing:

Those who beat their swords into ploughshares will end up ploughing for those who don't.

Just ask the Spartans' helots.

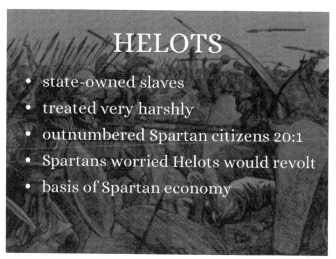

But our noble Families avoided such a miserable fate and accumulated Capital and Power via Private Profit. They used Myth and Money to manipulate and subjugate every Human Race. By the 1990s their Dream was Real—with the Russian race subjugated, the Chinese workforce enslaved and every human paying the price of Usury.

Though no river remains the same. All things change and now the greatest and most noble Family has put their man in the Oval Office, the Rothschild Family. For what reason we shall soon see.

The question of what is Right is only answered between equals; and The Families are without Equal.

The Peasants Have No Clothes

"The World" has been "saved" twice by bureaucrats so say the media. Recently when "the master" Bernanke "saved the World" from The Great Financial Crisis, and in 1997 when Time saw fit to call Rubin, Summers, and Greenspan, "The Committee To Save The World"; instead of calling them what they really were, namely the "Committee That Saved Wall Street" at the expense of Asia's teeming poor, who saw their national assets sold off for a pittance in order to pay back Wall Street oligarchs.

The trail of disaster in Alan Greenspan's wake just gets bigger and bigger. Testifying before Congress in 1997, Greenspan attributed the "extraordinary" and "exceptional" performance of the nineties economy to "a heightened sense of job insecurity" among workers "and, as a consequence, subdued wages." Alan Greenspan's traumatised worker is today's Trump supporter. They have been traumatised for 25 years so are in a pretty bad way, well done Alan. "An apocalypse on two legs" would be a fitting description for your legacy—And what a legacy!

The incubus of which began in the '60s, when the elite had a vision of a globalised economy based on a very harsh capitalism being promoted by Milton Freidman. Essentially, what was called 'Liberal Democracy' was the bringing together of two mutually exclusive ideas:

- Economic Liberalism – that enriches the few and impoverishes the many

- Democracy – that requires the support of the majority

A new world order based on economic liberalism was embraced by those at the top and despised by those at the bottom. From its early trial in Chile, it was known that economic liberalism, also known as Neo-Liberalism, and democracy did not sit well together; a military dictatorship was needed so democracy was set aside. It was brought to developing nations by selling its ideas directly to those at the top who would benefit from this ideology and who could impose it on those at the bottom by whatever means necessary.

The mass migrations of today are from those nations that have had economic liberalism imposed on them, like Eastern Europe, Africa and South America. They have been unable to escape through democracy and emigration was their only way out. In the West it has been imposed by stealth, with gradual progress over time, with the Right and Left undertaking different parts of the program:

- The Right undertake the tilting of the playing field in favour of the wealthy and away from the poor.

- The Left undertake the removal of ethnic and national identity with mass immigration and multiculturalism.

While those at the top were busy enjoying their profits they "maintained power ... by playing one part against the other ... to prevent all from having a common feeling." So listening to the population—Democracy—was never part of the plan. According to ideology they were part of Plato's elite and the population were just pig ignorant populists, so why listen to them? The word "liberal" was used as cover for the implementation of this harsh capitalism, with its pleasant and reasonable connotations.

It was so harsh it was felt it could only be trialled by military dictatorships in South America where torture, killing and brutality could be used to deal with the opposition that was usually tantamount to cleansing of any left wing thinking. Margaret Thatcher got the ball rolling in the West, she liked the look of this Capitalism that concentrated wealth amongst a few and brought wide spread poverty to the many. She was mean but lucky—the political economy of the United Kingdom was in disarray until North Sea oil put the class war to sleep.

Thatcher assumed power in 1980 and left office in 1990, what a lucky lady. She was literally battling unions in Wapping in '84 until oil boosted wages and calmed things down.

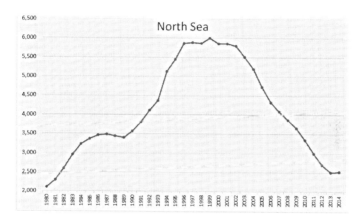

Empowered by new oil revenue, Margaret Thatcher went as far as she could get away with, although Milton Friedman wanted her to go much further as he had done in Chile. She later thanked General Pinochet for trialling this version of Capitalism, not mentioning the killing, torture and brutality that accompanied it. Pinochet was also an annual visitor to her home in London after he stepped down from power in 1990, always sending flowers and chocolates on his arrival in England. Days before his arrest for torture, conspiracy to torture and murder he was invited for tea at the former premier's home. Lady Thatcher campaigned vigorously for his release by reminding us of our "debt" to him and for "bringing democracy to Chile."

The ideal was to remove all Government services and welfare programs so they could be provided by the private sector for profit. All public companies should also be privatised. It has been progressing towards this goal ever since. In the West it had to be done by stealth, bit by bit, but was done far more brutally elsewhere. A PC thought police were trained up in every nation in Europe to denounce anyone against mass immigration as racist and xenophobic. It worked for a long time.

The same ideas were rolled out throughout America and as the nightmare vision became more and more apparent the breakdown began in the same way everywhere. The far right and left sprung up in Europe—Trump and Sanders in the US, UKIP and Corbyn in the UK—leading to Brexit and the death of TPP.

Next is Italy, Scottish Independence and The EURO.

The putative "father of the Euro", economist Robert Mundell is reported to have explained to one of his university of Chicago students, Greg Palast: "the Euro is the easy way in which Congresses and Parliaments can be stripped of all power over monetary and fiscal policy. Bothersome democracy is removed from the economic system."

What lovely people.

He aimed to remove democracy from the economic system. But with this design aim the Euro could not work as a currency. Like so much else, the entire EU project was meant to be Bait and Switch. First start with a common currency and promise it'll never go further than free trade. Then later, when in crisis, get everyone to agree to give up sovereignty and become The United States of Europe—essentially a centralised system of debt creation and allocation.

The Doom Loop was a design feature of the Euro. And for that we can thank the deplorable caste of professors of economy and their religion—Neo-Liberalism. Any good religion is lasting but Trump suggests this trash won't be round much longer.

To understand the Doom Loop one must first appreciate that a FIAT currency system is quite malleable and so there are three possible designs which allow government to finance a deficit:

1) The monetary system can be designed so the central bank is not independent from the government. Thus, when the government is stuck for money it can call on its central bank. The central bank creates the money and gives it to the government in the form of a loan, and the government spends

it. In an economic crisis such spending will be directed toward labour intensive activities to ameliorate distressed workers without an income. This approach may expand the supply of money and be inflationary, but please note that such a possible framework makes government quite powerful. And such power may be required to counter enemy action by bankers.

Essentially, bankers have the power to opt for monetary deflation (a reduction in the money supply) because it increases both the value of the money that they control and the interest rates that they can charge borrowers. However, they may abandon the deflationary idea in favour of inflating the money supply (which they accomplish by issuing bank loans) because of their eagerness to lend money at interest.

Bankers can gain an extra form of profit from this supposed conflict—by increasing the money supply with loans they increase the indebtedness of others and drive prices up. Then, by decreasing the money supply, they can force many debtors into foreclosure and confiscate whatever collateral was pledged to secure their loans. This manipulation of the money supply is a prominent aspect of the so-called "business cycle" and is destructive to business and industry and played a prominent role in the "panic of 1907".

Acting in concert, the big banks can also take out the competition. But if the government can monetise a deficit with its central bank, it can counter such power plays by bankers.

2) The government can borrow from foreigners—the IMF, World Bank and foreign banks are examples of such lenders—which may lend in foreign currency. This carries exchange rate risk as the loan may need to be repaid in a currency the government can't issue.

3) The third option is to borrow in your own currency by issuing government bonds. A bond is a promise to pay the holder of the bond a certain amount at the date of maturity. The Euro system was designed with this possibility in mind: European governments would borrow off private banks known as primary dealers—they buy the bonds. The bond can be sold on to sovereign wealth funds, insurance companies, mutual funds etc. with the banks making a cut on every transaction.

The Euro was designed in the days when Neo-Liberal economic ideas were all the rage and their problems had not come home to roost:

In the past, European governments could borrow from their Central Banks at low rates and use this facility in times of trouble for fiscal stimulus. We saw this in Latin America prior to and during the 1980's. The new Neo-Liberal thinking thought that Governments were reckless and inefficient and the private sector was sensible and efficient. Governments naturally take on too much debt to engage in wasteful spending to bribe voters. With this thinking in mind, it would be better if Governments **were forced** to borrow off private sector banks that would ensure that Government borrowing and spending was carried out efficiently under the watchful eye of the prudent private sector.

In 2008, we discovered the private banking sector was wild and reckless and that strong and robust Government was needed to bail the banks out. The thinking behind the design of the Euro was already unravelling rapidly.

As private banks held all the Government debt and the banks themselves were found to be insolvent, a doom loop was set up where Governments had to borrow off private banks to bail out those very same banks that had recklessly taken on bad debt in housing booms—e.g. Ireland, UK, Spain, Greece etc.

Policy makers have shown since 2008 that they have no confidence in the private sector to get things going again in a downturn. The private sector is there to make a profit and not risk potential losses in difficult times.

Policy makers first looked to Central Banks to use monetary policy to get things going again—they began to buy bonds from the banks—with the unstated goal of getting a polarised and apathetic population to agree to debt mutualisation.

After eight years this has failed everyone except bankers. And because the banks knew they'd buy anything and everything a form of financialised communism has emerged. Policy makers then looked to fiscal policy from Governments to get things going again, Governments that had been dismissed as reckless and inefficient in the design of the Euro. Unfortunately, the Euro was designed in the days when the private sector was thought to be the answer to all problems and is not designed to allow Governments much latitude with fiscal policy—they can't borrow from their Central Bank—so the design result is "austerity".

Also known as plunder of national assets and money scarcity (monetary deflation) which resulted in sky high unemployment and seizure of collateral in exchange for foreign funding of deficits.

Amazing. Hundreds of millions of Europeans left to the mercy of flawed and evil ideas.

The Great Financial Crisis and subsequent bail-in of taxpayer money drew back the curtain on outright criminality by the elite and duplicity on the part of mainstream media. (See The Inside Job or The Big Short for an excellent artistic overview.) The crisis was too unstable and austerity so severe that the masses rejected the brainwash— a biblical flood of propaganda about the benefits of mutual debt began in 2009. One cannot recall a single news article —out of thousands about the benefits of centralised debt—that asked why a German worker would want a foreign politician to be able to borrow money in his name? Why would the elite want a government that could borrow in the name of all 550 million Europeans? What if the elite captured that one government?

And why would such a government be so desirable to capture? Could one reason be because it CAN borrow other people's money in your name and give it to the owners of the government? Like what happened in 2008 when bureaucrats in Washington gave Trillions of public debt—your future taxes—to bankers?

Could it be that the bankers are the elite?

As things happened the elite got the crisis they wanted but the masses dug in their heels and refused to accept 'the switch' of centralised debt and power. So the revolt did not begin with Brexit, it began when European citizens refused mutual debt and a super state, whereby German taxpayers would be on the hook for Portuguese debt and vice versa.

The international elite can't seem to understand why their dream hasn't gone down so well. Maybe some are totally unaware that their dream is actually a nightmare for most lower down the ladder. They don't mix with them or have anything to do with them, so how would they know? As it became more and more obvious what is going on in the West, the "liberal" cover was blown and everyone tries to get away from a thoroughly unreasonable centre. The far right and far left in Europe rejecting shared debt and federalism, Trump in the US and Farage leading to Brexit. As the story unfolds we might well ask "What morons thought an ideology that had to be trialled in a military dictatorship would work with democracy?"

"We need names," I hear you cry. Here are some names for you: Robert Rubin, former Goldman Sachs CEO. When he was Clinton's Secretary of the Treasury he rammed through the Riegle-Neal Act, the Gramm-Leach-Bliley Act and the Commodities Futures Modernization Act of 2000. Those acts gave the too big to fail banks interstate banking, killed the Glass-Steagall Act and deregulated derivatives. With that, those banks were given total control of the US economy after causing the greatest economic crash since the Great Depression. During the crash, Goldman Sachs CEO Hank Paulson become the new Secretary of the Treasury. Paulson gave us the Emergency Economic Stabilization Act of 2008, which gifted bankers with generational wealth, while stripping savers and pensioners of the interest on their savings, and sending pension plans down the road to insolvency.

A grand folly has been playing out for decades and begins to draw to a close —the mainstream media calls it pig ignorant populism but the truth, dear reader, is that "behind closed doors, the FED Chairs are terrified." The platonic 'elite' are just as dumb as the next person, but Milton Friedman told them greed was good.

And dumbasses never question their priests.

Desperate Measures
by Oil expert Sapere Aude

How much money are they making on shale.

Answers to the nearest zero please.

Yet again, the perceived strength of shale is its downfall. Yes, being tight geology allows drillers using horizontal drilling and hydraulic fracking to start off like taking the bubbles from a shaken coca cola bottle... you get a lot out... to start with, but then the fizz goes pretty damned quick.

It's not technological advancement either, as hydraulic fracking has been around for decades and decades. The biggest change was pad drilling, but even that cannot defy physics. The basic concept about shale drilling is it can drill laterally and frack formations that otherwise could not produce oil, but doing it, means that the laterals and the fracking exhaust the oil or gas very quickly indeed.

Look at the Bakken decline, then look at other shale plays that had their reserves over-estimated by 80%. And then look at all the old legacy wells on the Bakken, producing next to nothing, but leaving a legacy of leakage and blighted land, because companies prefer to keep them running at a loss than pay the cost of properly plugging and abandoning them.

Decline rates in the region of 70% in the first year. Eagle Ford is on its back ready to die now, too, and everyone running to the next Ponzi—the Permian—shall suffer the same fate:

Red Queen Syndrome.

That is, you drill 1000 wells at 1,000 barrels of oil per day (bopd), and you get 1,000,000bopd Initial Peak Production... within days that starts to drop off, and by six months you've already lost 50% of your production, giving you just 500,000bopd but you keep the cost of sustaining the 1,000 wells, so you need another 500 wells drilled at 6 month period just to keep production at the original peak of 1,000,000bopd.

At the end of the year you have the original 1,000 wells declined by 65% minimum, so the original 1,000,000 from them is now just 350,000bopd, but now you have also got the legacy effect on the 500 six month old wells that were doing 500,000, but are now doing 250,000 so you are down to 600,000bopd after the first year. So you have to drill another 600 wells to make up for the decline, but each day the decline rates on these and the other wells mount up… and that is what Red Queen Syndrome is.

If peak oil was not true, we would not even be drilling shale wells, nor tackling oil sands, nor using sour oil, or using enhanced recovery techniques. But we are, because we need all the oil we can find, and the only reason the glowing picture of an oil glut is put out, is to convince everyone else of how cheap oil should be, to keep the price down, aided by a myriad of oil futures contracts. The US wants to import oil on the cheap.

Not so long ago sour oil was not even in the world oil production figures, because it was not even saleable, NOW IT REPRESENTS THE MAJORITY OF ALL OIL PRODUCED.

Likewise, enhanced oil recovery would not be undertaken if oil was so easy and plentiful, but it is now in the majority and more worrying still is the super giant fields which are not being replaced, that are all in terminal decline, which is why the Saudis wants to get the punters in.

They've not produced accurate depletion rates for years, and I don't expect the IPO will either. Ghawar has been subject to WATER FLOODING, a sure sign of it being in terminal decline and once that decline sets in production plummets never to recover, even with more and more money being thrown at it. How much do you think it costs to water flood the Ghawar field in the middle of a desert where water is so expensive. Is it because there's a glut?

Just take a look at some of the Super Giant Fields where super giant fields are not being discovered, hence going for everything we can find, including deep sea and shale, and even oil sands, the most dangerous of all oils ecologically.

Ghawar, Saudi Arabia, production started 1951, rumoured to have peaked in 2005.

Burgan Field, Kuwait, production started 1948, peaked 2005.

Gachsaran Field, Iran, production started 1930, peaked 1974.

Canterell Field, Mexico, production started 1981, peaked 2004.

Ahwaz Field, Iran, production started 1954, peaked 1970s.

Do you know the Ghawar Oil field alone has produced around 51,000,000,000bbls and it provided 60-65% of all Saudi oil. Do you know how much water they have to use now to get a fast declining output, 7,000,000 gallons a day, not bad for a desert country!

The water cut alone is now 46%. Look below and wake up.

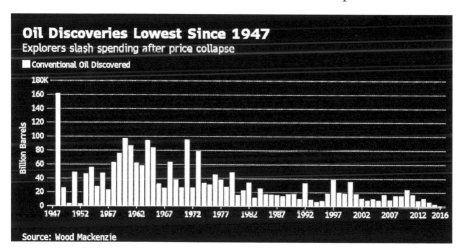

So many people don't want to look at the facts, they want to believe in fairies.

Next comes the fake pictures of fake tankers full of oil, photo-shopped and then purported to be off Iran, then the same picture used as being off Galveston, but whoever put the picture together made the mistake of using cargo ships, tankers, oil tankers, chemical carriers, and worst of all—many were showing their plimsoll mark which meant they were empty.

Amateurs!

No one wants the shale. Who wants to buy into shale when no company ever made a profit. Its basic physics at work that show shale companies are bust, so it amazes me to see people commenting about $20 oil, when the shale companies couldn't make a profit at $80. Look at their horrendous figures.

Peak oil is a proven thesis, unfortunately it's the ignorant who quote it without realising what Peak Oil referred to, and at what point in history it was made, and where historically Peak Oil has been proven to have passed.

If it wasn't can anyone tell me why we are using sour oil? When we never used to use it before, because there was no market for it.

Can anyone tell me why we are drilling deep in offshore dangerous locations?

Can anyone tell me why virtually all the Super Giant Fields are being subjected to enhanced recovery and multiple methods of recovery and work-overs to eke out more oil?

Can anyone tell me why we are bothering to utilise Canadian oil sands, the most destructive and cost ineffective oil out there?

Can anyone tell me why they are working on the Permian now?

It's because they have used up the sweet spots elsewhere, on the Eagle Ford, the Bakken, the Monterey and for the record, NONE OF THEM CAME NEAR TO THE RESERVES THE EIA ATTRIBUTED TO THEM.

There are only finite drilling sites on the acreage and pads and the geology only supports a finite number of wells before well saturation decreases the output from ANY subsequent well, and then you run out of sweet spots.

Then you have the 1000's of wells after a few years that are nothing more than stripper wells, producing as little as 30bopd and costing more for the infrastructure and maintenance, they badly need plugging and abandoning as they are not profitable and are poisoning the land, but then no company wants to admit they only lasted that long, or cough up the $2m per well to properly plug them.

What's with all the climate change propaganda? Climate change is ONE BIG CON. Pure hyperbole. If you don't believe me, take a look at 'Al Gore's Inconvenient Truth', watch it and carefully mark down all the horrific results we were going to see. NOT ONE OF THEM CAME INTO BEING. And he got a Nobel Prize (from The Powers That Be). That must have helped the sheep believe him. What a joke. It even became a mini Religion.

This is all to wean us off oil that is not going to be available to everyone, there's not even enough to go around now. How do you think Syria and all the other countries racked by war will be rebuilt? In all likelihood, they won't be. Greece was just the first western nation to be systematically targeted for artificial repression; so they were no longer able to demand as much oil.

Now let us take a proper look at oil shall we?

20 years ago, the oil market was based on sweet oil. Heavy and sour oil were discarded as there was no market for such low quality product. Today the majority of the world's oil produced falls into these categories. The easy stuff has already been exploited hence shale reared its Ponzi head.

But let's not stop there, let's take a look at shale shall we.

It was 4,000,000bbls peak and now dropping, as the sweet spots have all been drilled and there are only a finite number of wells you can drill in any space. Let us then consider Canadian oil tar, the most ecologically damaging of all oil, about 3,000,000bbls. Again, none of that figured in previous years. So between them we have 7,000,000bbls a day of production (with shale dropping). So what would happen without that 7,000,000bbls a day?

Currently the world uses up, even with countries at war and in artificially induced recession, around 98,000,000bbls a day. Take 7,000,000 from that... WHO IS GOING TO GO WITHOUT?

Then consider depletion rates on that 98,000,000bbls a day. In order to keep 98,000,000bbls a day new wells have to be drilled to make up for depletion and decline.

The World Energy Outlook report of 2007 discussed decline and depletion rates for the first time. The IEA included in its analysis a study of the depletion rates of the world's top 800 oil fields: 6.7% for past-peak fields, increasing to 8.6% by 2030. Averaged across all fields, the rate was 5.1%, but that included 3.4% for the very largest fields, 6.5% for the next-largest and then 10.4%.

But these are only the "observed decline rates." The authors distinguish that from a "natural decline rate," which "strips out the effects of ongoing and periodic investment". The authors note that the natural decline rates "are about a third higher on average than observed decline rates," with a global average of about 9% in 2007.

If you were generous and said 90,000,000bbls of the oil produced daily was from conventional wells, that still leaves a year on year decline in output from 90,000,000bbls to 82,800,000bbls a day. SO WHO IS GOING TO GO WITHOUT?

That's not the complete picture though, as shale production of 4,000,000 declines in the first year to just 1,200,000bbls a day, so who is going to go without that oil?

So overall we have decline rates per year on oil of around 10,000,000bbls a day production. Production gets harder and harder to achieve as field saturation occurs. So who is going to go without? And what will happen when *the debt fails*? What did economists mean when they said "the debt will fail" if Trump gets elected. They never specified what that meant. Probably because they don't have a clue. The Bankers know what will happen though. Let me tell you:

A number of costs are built into the price of any good. Some costs, such as addiction, pollution, cancer, depletion and destruction of the ecological system are not included and hopefully some other sap is forced to suffer them —and pay the cost of my profit. The cost of labour, energy, communication, government and usury is built into consumer prices. Since Financial Elites in the US went full FIAT in the 1970s the cost of usury began to increase at an exponential rate—due to the compounding promises to pay interest.

You can see this clearly if you look at house price charts since then. The prices had to inflate to include the compounding cost of usury. The cost of usury began to compound because the debt was never cleared-out or forgiven. The result was predictable, the price of assets in existence began to hyper-inflate across the entire Planet.

Capital markets in the West were flush with petrodollars after '74, hence the desire by banks to make Dollar loans. Third world countries were reclassified as 'emerging-markets' and were flooded with Dollars, which the local Dominant Class could access. Some local currencies couldn't take it and collapsed repeatedly, such as the Mexican Peso, with their Oligarchs using the hard currency to then buy up all the farming land from the financially distressed peasants. It's as if another round of Conquest occurred, with the displaced natives fleeing to US prison systems. Most US cities are now little more than huge warehouses for the reserve army of labour.

If the debt fails the built-up cost of usury will be removed from asset prices and then there will be a MASSIVE deflationary shock (when measured against real money.) The price of a house will return to its historical average, somewhere between 6 to 48 months of labour income.

Think about it, how many man hours does it take to build a house? 2 carpenters could build a house in 6 weeks and then all you need is payment for materials, piping, wiring, plumbing and furnishings.

Now take a moment to imagine the political consequences. That is why the FED chairs are terrified.

Next stage, all below cost oil production will cease due to the return to harder money. So no more shale or tar oil sands. That's around 7,000,000 barrels of oil that will disappear instantly. So who is going to go without?

And then you have the real black swan to add to that—THE TAX TAKE.

A gramme of petrol contains as much energy as a gramme of explosives and that's why we need hydrocarbons as the energy punch is so good. For every gallon of diesel the tax take is approximately 27.3 cents. For gasoline it's 26.60

cents per gallon. Now multiply that by 384,740,000 gallons a day gasoline use. That figure then gets slaughtered each time, with a double whammy of subsidies for green energy, so government budgets are screwed up beyond belief in an act of self-annihilation.

It's impossible for US oil production to have increased simply by virtue of the rate of decline of legacy wells. More drawdowns from the Strategic Petroleum Reserve (SPR) to the wellhead to artificially manipulate production is losing credibility as more and more realise manipulation on a grand scale, just like the paper gold and paper silver. You don't have 695 million barrels in the SPR, it's been drawn down using the bidirectional pipelines the SPR was built with.

It was built to be bidirectional for a reason, to allow discrete use of oil in the SPR, and for the last 18 months oil has been flowing from the SPR to the wellheads and then being stated as US production where production figures are fictional and have to be due to laws of physics, where shale wells deplete by 70% in the first year.

You watch, and remember this, when now in order to balance the books of oil that has already been used from the SPR but unpublicised, the government will have to announce a sale of oil from the SPR, but where that oil (a bit like the Gold market) no longer exists anyway, so the only way out is a fictional sale of oil that isn't there anyway.

[Updated in January, 2017] It's such a pity so many are so thick. Last year I mentioned the US would be forced to sell from the SPR just to balance the books. They have been using the bidirectional pipelines to artificially boost production in wells, by counting drawdowns from the SPR, so then they had to announce a sale of 8 million barrels, because they've already consumed them.

More dodgy figures and yet some of you actually believe them. Gold, Silver, Oil, all subject to the same manipulation, yet some believe the Gold and silver manipulation but won't consider crude oil is being manipulated by bloating the US production figures and the inventory builds, not by minor amounts but by epic proportions as the shales fail. The only thing that is in a glut, in both Oil, Gold and Silver, are little bits of paper produced by US commodity exchanges, with a level of leverage that is ridiculous, just like the 100oz of paper gold for every ounce that actually exists!!

The same is true for silver and oil, it's the paper that's running the markets, but the world knows it. This garbage constantly coming out about increased production, when the decline of legacy wells means it's a real struggle to even maintain production, is just ridiculous and anyone involved in shale knows it.

So these fictional figures of production increases are provably false, see <u>Red Queen Syndrome</u>. The petrodollar is backed by the oil we control and as the economic value of our oil dies so too does the Petrodollar. This death is visible if you know what to look for: the Eurodollar market is dying from a lack of dollars. That right there is the physical limit of the PONZI. And we've hit the physical limit.

That's why those Russian Fields are so precious.

Appendix: Reader, please note that Goldman Sachs, via President Trump, declared the sale of half the Strategic Petroleum Reserve in May, 2017.

The Cost of Capitalism

The market is past, present and future possibility. There's just not that many possibilities left.

History suggests Gold should be used only as an accounting currency between nation states. And the use of a neutral institution is required to ensure imbalances between trading nations are not prolonged. For if a nation must deliver physical Gold as substitute for trading loss the surplus nation shall have an incentive to prolong the imbalance until the debtor is removed of all Gold. Such monetary arrangement would be short lived and nationalistic; poison trading relations and result in war and acrimony. This was the system flaw leading up to World War One.

The Economy will be shrinking due to Depletion so a complex financial system will not be required. Only a fraction of the population will be required for production since automation and AI will continue to advance. Gold will only be used by major players for trade and only claims of ownership will change. There is a lot of wealth accumulated that can't be demanded by money in circulation, as almost all wealth is not for sale on any given week. It'll be interesting to see if the FIAT price of Gold represents such. Gold is money, though it is also not in circulation.

Then there is banker credit and lawful money in circulation. Such money has a FIAT stamp, a number. All FIAT money in circulation represents the ability to demand all goods and services that are for sale. Lawful money will keep the market moving and enable a Basic Income. The prices of all goods and services exchanged within the currency area will automatically inflate to match the FIAT in circulation.

If too much FIAT is printed, then the Gold price in that currency will inflate, thus ensuring that the FIAT creators can't corner the Gold Market. All accumulated wealth and value will struggle against entropy, an increasing share of remaining energy sources will be directed to struggle against this phenomenon. That's why arable land, forestry and Gold ownership is so important; their value is not as exposed to entropy as other asset classes.

The carrying capacity of the planet is around 4-5 Billion without oil. We can anticipate a minimum population reduction of 30% since oil provides a third of our energy. The supply of natural gas and coal may increase to soften the blow, but the oceans are also dying, which is most worrying as fish is a major source of protein for humans. The unofficial leadership may be tempted to use The Reset as cover to radically reduce the population.

One of the generally unstated reasons the bank bail-outs occurred in 2008 was because if the financial system had collapsed international trade would have ceased instantly. No ships would have set sail because international trade requires letters of credit and insurance, which are managed by the Financial System.

Also, one should note that the banks couldn't be broken up after the heart attack because the value of their parts were not what they were claimed to be. The banks were lying, their assets were marked to fantasy and Central Banking authorities knew this as they had the real data.

The Financial System is essentially the Operating System for the global economy; without which all trade would cease immediately. The average city has 3 days of food supplies. Without trade the population would starve, exit the cities in search of food and then there would be general mayhem and chaos. If a nation has no functional Financial System trade may be cut off. Once the water pumps fail there would be mass death.

Such mass behaviour carries extinction risk. There are 4,000 pools of spent-nuclear fuel in countries like India, Pakistan, Algeria, Ukraine etc. Just a single pool at Fukushima:

"The No. 4 unit was not operating at the time of the accident, so its fuel had been moved to the pool from the reactor, and if you calculate the amount of cesium 137 in the pool, the amount is equivalent to 14,000 Hiroshima atomic bombs," said Hiroaki Koide, assistant professor at Kyoto University Research Reactor Institute.

Extinction is baked in if The Reset goes awry or America's hegemonic system collapses in an unplanned fashion. Most of the Middle East would descend into civil war due to deep seated hate, and tribal and sectarian vendettas. After the crisis breaks formerly rich nations may be extremely violent. The native populations shall be just north of survival and they'll direct their rage at visible targets. Recent immigrants and racial minorities promised milk and butter shall riot. The sociopathic leaders may encourage the masses to direct their rage at the burdensome outsiders. They'll most likely be expelled or exterminated by the enraged masses.

Those nations with no Gold should be avoided. Without Gold to recapitalise their Financial Systems such nations shall have an extremely hard time surviving. They may be targeted by hegemonic powers for population reduction.

Only the industrialised core needs to be protected for the continuance of Culture. Culture is social peer-pressure which trains vocal actions by adjusting them until they are socially acceptable. The adjusted vocal muscle patterns are stored in unconscious memory as muscle activation patterns. That's why your primary school teacher made you drill multiplication tables and phonic sounds when you were a child. Words have no meaning. They are simply muscle activation patterns that allow you to access the Culture, where all meaning resides.

The sentence tells the listener what action he's meant to do: "That'll be 10 dollars please" tells you to hand over a 10 dollar note. "It's getting late" tells you you're meant to take your date home. Such sentences put pressure on you to react in harmony with established norms. All human knowledge gets stored in our ratcheting Culture, so the brain needs no representations or computations. This is energy efficient.

No knowledge of how to do something is in our heads, but is in the Culture. We do not build a model of the world in our heads. We access the Culture by means of vocal muscle actions, and outsource all other functions to the cultural cloud. This allows humans to be on the same evolutionary path as all other mammals. The algorithm cycles at 10-100 Hz, while the conscious, perceptual leg adjusts the unconscious muscle-pattern memory. The interface between perception and muscle pattern memory allows images to be stored as muscle activation patterns in the unconscious.

Now the body is conscious, with instant recall of image patterns stored as muscle activation patterns. This algorithm interlocks present perception with past perception and experience, thus adding a sense of continuity to the self.

Even as a person's appearance and social role changes he still feels attached to the person that he was. He automatically responds to a given stimulus with the same muscle activation pattern. If he perceives the right body shape his body will respond automatically. And addiction forms if pleasure is the end result.

Neurons are energetically expensive, the brain uses 20% of all energy as the nervous system prioritises inputs, your teacher said the words 'Pay attention!' so you would prioritise her output. A frog that can't ignore the pain in its leg when its eye is signalling that a large shadow is passing overhead gets eaten. And a frog that has to be simultaneously "aware" of the pain and the shadow is likely to starve to death.

Thus, the space that humans share will always become mono-cultural through time in order for the individual brain to conserve energy, access meaning and know-how, and reduce the risk and stress of miscommunication. Those brains that can't cope with the complexity of the Culture are automatically excluded from the Dominant Religion—Capitalistic societies send them to private prisons, killing fields, university or give them drugs—they are "the labour problem."

So you'll notice that almost all companies produce one good or service well. If it does two things a break up usually adds value. And with time a company will form its own language or slang: phrasal sentences such as 'Do a bear hug,' 'You need to lean in,' 'Pass the book at 7' are senseless to you and me for our brain was never exposed to the Culture—accumulated knowledge/social peer pressure—that they reference.

During the Dark Ages, work was by the job. A wealthy man, say a priest or landlord, would gather local peasants to build a wall or take in the harvest. Then they would get paid and disband. The concept of *company* was an important civilizational breakthrough: as the workforce was permanently employed in a company, a company Culture formed in which all know-how inhered. The company Culture is the vehicle that drove and stored the explosive growth in Mankind's knowledge. The internet stores data and information. Usually, disruption of an industry or incumbent company is caused by new knowledge. Capitalism is the recursive process of knowledge accumulation whereby God shall come to know Himself.

All knowledge is stored within the Culture of Religion. Understanding is external to such—Philosophy.

My main point is that knowledge of production when confined and enclosed within a given space with competitive and continuous financial pressure, created a continuous culture within which inhered the working knowledge of the company. The company culture is experienced by the worker as social peer pressure—pressure that shapes his behaviour to be efficient and complaisant to authority. The brain of the average human worker, barely more intelligent than a chimp, does not need to model any solutions since it can simply learn to respond to the company culture. Culture is social peer pressure—which every human and animal brain has evolved to respond to in a pack and tribal setting. Thus, the company culture was a good fit for the human brain at carrying knowledge of production as it was neurologically efficient. Even if an ingenious worker died his innovations lived on in the company culture.

Only a tiny minority of workers are required to model novel solutions because only a tiny minority of humans have the mental powers to do so—and their solutions become part of the working Culture which all workers can access.

Capitalism achieved universal status because it benefited the sociopaths the most. It could produce more goods since it stored and transmitted more knowledge than competing religions. Especially working knowledge pertaining to production. And interestingly you can observe superseded religions adapt their dogma so more goods can be delivered to their leaders. For example, the Vatican now has its own bank that uses usury, and recent Popes were said to be quite taken with Capitalism.

Almost all religions have capitalistic traits today. And they come and go. Some have deities and others do not. They are easily seen as they are about power. An interesting example in our age was when Freud and Jung used the language of metaphysics to develop Psychoanalysis. A body of knowledge was produced by these learned men whose calling was the understanding and treatment of the crippling misery of psycho-emotional pain. Their efforts were largely harmless and with time the laity gave them the status of authority. This attracted the sociopaths who wanted power—of particular note is nephew Bernays and daughter—Anna Freud.

She used her apparent success at treating the children of Dorothy Burlingham to gain power and control over the psychoanalytic movement. She wanted the world to accept her ideas and vision of human behaviour. Her advocacy went swimmingly and in 1946 Truman signed the National Mental Health Act.

Until the sheep stopped believing the bullshit. No bullshit. No Power. No point. Am I right?

"Well, firstly, psychoanalysis fell out of favour. It became impossible to hide the fact that it just didn't work. Some famous patients, like Marilyn Monroe, committed suicide. Anna Freud was discredited too. One of the Burlingham children, whose analysis had apparently been so successful, actually came back from America as an adult and committed suicide in Freud's London house, where Anna still lived."

It appears that modern media—due to advertising—is adept at producing new religions and is also good at destroying them.

Given the above, the industrialised core shall most likely be protected as all working knowledge inheres within its Culture. Nations without energy resources should be avoided; food importers should be avoided. Nations without a high calibre nuclear defence should be avoided. And finally, multiracial nations should be avoided—humans have not evolved beyond the tribe—and the peasants may kill each other. The Dominant Class know this and have sought to maintain their power in recent years by dividing the population by importing foreign bodies, and then playing one part against the other.

Message received April, 2017:

Conquest of Russia has failed.
All Muscovite fifth column agents cleaned out.
Putrid's thesis, that the Age of Capitalism has ended, is true.
The Families have decided to make major changes to money flows.
Cryptos can perform as currency.

Reader, watch the Crypto prices. If they go to the moon, it's time.

Aggression or Death

Rothschild: War is profitable, Putrid

Putrid: Not when the wages are paid in precious metal.

Rothschild: The key is to win and then you decide what constitutes payment.

Putrid: The cheaper the payment the better?

Rothschild: Humans will use anything that provides a competitive advantage—it's the way Nature made us—cheaper is just another word for more efficiency. Debt, bullshit, drugs—all very efficient.

Putrid: Only if they're told it's a competition.

Rothschild: A resource constrained world is pretty competitive.

Putrid: True.

Rothschild: Is there anything we're missing?

Putrid: Maybe we're not seeing the most important reality. Which is, what exists in the mind of our fellow men.

Rothschild: And whether what exists is reasonable.

Putrid: How can it be reasonable when everything we tell them is false?

Rothschild: Reasonable… Tell me the nature of Reason, Putrid.

Putrid: It appears orderly.

Rothschild: So it can govern the future.

Putrid: How can you govern the unknown? How does the unknown become orderly?

Rothschild: Use the Law. The laws of the land shape mass behaviour, producing expectations and social peer pressure.

Putrid: Yes, but the Law only governs predictable problems and conflicts.

Rothschild: But common sense lets us choose the least evil option when we happen upon rare circumstances.

Putrid: True for the peasants. Not true for you. The Future—big F, System

Level—is unknown.

Rothschild: But the path that results in the least amount of suffering is the best path to take.

Putrid: Perhaps at the local level where predictions are feasible. But there's no morality at the System Level. Knowledge precedes moral feeling—so at the local level, if you see an injured child, you feel moved to help—the knowledge preceded the feeling. But at the System Level, no knowledge of the Future exists. We don't know what the ultimate result is of doing nothing; of nuking Russia; of triggering The Reset, etcetera. And whatever path is chosen, the further down the causal chain, the more uncertain the ultimate result becomes.

Rothschild: If an outcome is uncertain, then it's unknown.

Putrid: Correct.

R: Some actions are evil, their very nature is evil. We ought to eschew them.

Putrid: True. And if we follow this principle you should do nothing. And according to our preferred models the global economy will disintegrate, unravelling the market, resulting in the extinction of humankind.

Rothschild: So the least evil act results in the most suffering?

Putrid: Maybe. We don't know.

Rothschild: Reason and morality don't really fit, do they?

Putrid: Not for the Fathers of Religion. You're not responsible if knowledge of the ultimate result is not feasible.

Rothschild: So what's the function of Reason then?

Putrid: It produces an organised Mind. The organised absolute is conscious. The will wants power. You have power and it's organised—by Religion. Xi and Putin have a different religion. So it's a question of which religion wins.

The myth is for the children. Their will is directed toward the goodness the myth will bring. They want their myth to have power. They know it deeply that power is the ultimate good—for they are crippled by the feeling of powerlessness.

Rothschild: So they fantasize about having the power?

Putrid: To take a common myth, those that believe in the goodness of free market capitalism fantasize about the unfettered power they'll enjoy when they become The Capitalist.

Rothschild: But that's bullshit. I have the power.

Putrid: That's why it's a myth.

Rothschild: They can't see past their desire?

Putrid: They can't see past their fear.

Rothschild: What do they fear?

Putrid: Powerlessness to protect their children.

Rothschild: What's the point in Understanding?

Putrid: Inner peace. It's a beautiful feeling. There's me. There's Religion. There's God. That's it. Nothing else. The human mind is housed within Religion. That's where all the knowledge is. Now a carpenter knows how to hang a door. You're at the Top, so you know how to nuke Russia. How to pull off The Reset. How to destroy faith in the competing-

Rothschild: Going forward?

Putrid: Difficult situation. How to extract ever scarcer resources without the natives waking up?

Rothschild: Disinformation. Drugs.

Putrid: But decision makers at the Nation State level form policy using the same disinformation so there's more and more fuck ups. Which is destroying faith in the global government.

R: Why is that important? If the government is global where can they go?

Putrid: It is no longer global. The Competing System is stable.

Rothschild: An increasingly difficult balancing act. Keeping almost all humans ignorant while needing them to continue to actively support the System Framework.

Putrid: That's why the social peer pressure keeps getting harsher and harsher and more and more irrational, and the laws multiply. It's all top down with no comprehensive reasoning provided—so now there's passive and active resistance—nothing makes sense anymore so the masses are irritated and paranoid. And most importantly, this is making the local leaders scared, one of these days, they may move to save their own skin.

Rothschild: That can't happen in the sand-box.

Putrid: True, but the situation is even worse there. Larger and larger areas are running at a loss, rather than eat into "savings" that aren't there the locals need force to capture resources. Or be depopulated. And then there must be a point, perhaps already passed in many places, where the cost of Empire is greater than the gain.

Rothschild: How can that be measured?

Putrid: Critically important countries in the sand-box are running at a loss. That right there is your empirical measurement. Who, in their right mind, would finance a deficit for such nations? So it's aggression or death.

Rothschild: Or aggression and death. Thank God I'm not responsible.

Putrid: Putin doesn't care what God thinks. We can safely assume he holds The Families responsible for the Bolshevik Revolution and the weakening of Russia, which led to German aggression and the death of his brother and the hanging of his grandmother. And let's not forget the latest round of humiliation in the 90s.

Rothschild: Revenge is a Right?

Putrid: I think we both know that Russia's retaliation won't be directed at American infrastructure. Why would Putin want to kill some poor unfortunates that never harmed him and his loved ones. Why would the Russian leadership build the ability to trace the physical movements and location of every member of The Families and then bury such equipment deep underground Moscow? I think it's safe to assume that wherever The Families are located will receive the retaliation.

So, for the first time, The System, has put you and yours, and The Families, on the Menu.

Rothschild: You're enjoying this Putrid.

Putrid: Intensely so. I hear the big nukes leave a crater half a kilometre deep.

Meta-Analysis

When we speak of 'The System' we are simply referring to the framework of the capitalistic religion.

Far more beautiful is idea and mind—will and creation. The idea is order and consciousness. The will is creation, struggle and destruction. The cosmic process is between will and idea.

The Russians are conscious of their danger and the source of such. They know The Families would kill half of humanity to prolong their religion, this is clearly true given the historical record. So they have consciously ordered their economy to produce highly precise tactical cruise and strategic nuclear missiles—And the ability to trace the location of The Families.

So whichever way this war is waged—even if The Families demand warfare limited to conventional forces—the Russian leadership can instantly kill their children with cruise missiles wherever they are located.

Thus, for the very first time, the heads of The Families are powerless to protect their own children. They now struggle with the same fear that haunts their fellow men.

Unless one is born with a philosophical nature it must be difficult to comprehend and understand this new experience. They don't know how to proceed.

Because it appears to be mentally challenging to prepare for offensive war knowing that your own children will be amongst the first casualties.

Here we have a beautiful example of idea overcoming the will—to kill and conquer, to rape and rob. What a pleasure to watch the cosmic process in real time—to witness the World Spirit move to Russia.

We shall witness now whether the idea overcomes the will. And if it does the cosmic process shall progress furthermore—The Mind shall develop new understanding of Itself as AI adds new grades and textures to the Conscious Absolute.

Beautiful.

The Russian leadership and population are preparing for war. They know a big War is coming. And since 2014 have prepared for nothing else. They are ordered and conscious of the coming contest. They may win.

For the West isn't ready—nor are The Families.

On the other hand the West needs this war to survive.

The West is in a classic double bind. What do you do when you know your system is collapsing but you have no time left to adjust and to prepare for a war you desperately need to survive—while your opponent is prepared for everything?

And make no mistake—the Russians are prepared—for everything.

Operational Analysis

Putrid: It shall become increasingly difficult to maintain the appearance of growth going forward.

Deadwood: Keeping up appearances is no longer working. That's why the Fed will attempt to reduce financial risk by reigning in liquidity, but increase the RISK PARITY trade in the U.S. and global financial system, similar to the scenario that crushed Long Term Capital Management in September 1998. Hedge Funds are being set-up to take the wrath.

Putrid: Saudi and the wider Gulf Region require revenues now, so Qatar gas fields need to be seized.

Deadwood: Qatar is an EXON Mobile franchise. Nothing in Qatar gets decided without Exon approval. As for the Saudis----who cares?! They have outlived their existence.

Putrid: I'm told the Eurodollar Market is dying from a lack of dollars. I intuit they mean that less and less transactions are taking place using Dollars.

Deadwood: The offshore money market world is failing to produce collateral and this failure to produce collateral is reflected in the Eurodollar funding markets. QE doesn't address this problem as it is interest rate driven stimulus and this isn't a cost of capital problem but a collateral problem.

There is a chronic dollar shortage in financial markets because of the high dollar. Dollar denominated debts become increasingly unmanageable as hedging costs rise. This creates a feedback loop whereby in order to decrease risk, market participants either hedge dollar risk (where their collateral is in other currencies, but they have USD costs somewhere in their cost structure…think European manufacturers using US technology for example). These guys hedge this exposure by buying dollars, and this pushes the dollar higher, or market participants reduce leverage by unwinding debt positions, and in order to do so they have to buy back dollars as they unwind what are short dollar positions. Once again this pushes the dollar higher.

Putrid: The outlook for The Families is deteriorating fast. I suppose they could never have fathomed that Bo Xilai would be taken down by Secretary Xi and Putin would out-play them.

Deadwood: Xi and Putin are playing in another league. They didn't inherit their power. They got to the top by fighting. Xi is one among many "Princelings" and was gravely wounded by an assassin sent by Bo Xilai and his friends. One of whom, an MI6 asset, ended up dead in a hotel room. So Xi is a fighter—And a winner. The Families aren't used to this game play. The last one who played in this style was Joseph Stalin. And that didn't end well for your correspondents.

Putrid: They need to make a decision regarding Depopulation, these deficits countries are about to implode-explode.

Deadwood: How can they make a decision regarding Depopulation when they can't even agree where to relocate to?

Putrid: I thought they were more noble than this.

Deadwood: Hard to think straight when your children are the prey.

Being amoral is easy when there's no risk of retaliation. The last leader to put his own near the front line was Mao and it was a decision he regretted bitterly.

Putrid: What system role are the Cryptos playing?

I think business as usual will end the minute Crypto-currency generated profits are putting a bid under Gold. Those Crypto-currency profits are generated outside the controlled Central Bank FIAT Ponzi. It's obvious the Central Banks aren't seeing it & hadn't been informed. The Central Bank's desperate attempt to create a mechanism to control the in- and outflow on the CME through digital 'money flow systems' can't work anymore because of the 'decentralization' nature of Crypto-currencies. The Central Bank freaks have lost control of their own Ponzi.

This creates two possibilities which interweave into the Future:

A) The crypto-currencies are driven to the moon by profits which are then invested in Gold as a hedge against monetary collapse and a hyper-inflation mentality takes hold of investors and then the general population.

B) The Competing System—or The Families—consciously bid up the Crypto-currency price to trigger The Reset.

Extinction is the System Result

What a spectacle the peasants make, like children at their first circus, they cheered for Trump. A very entertaining pageant of manipulation, and then to watch the masses realize they were fooled once more. "Perhaps the snowflakes were right," they mutter darkly.

And this concluding piece is not a complaint on my part, the mass manipulation, and then the Reality dawning to crush the hope of countless millions—"Are you not entertained!?"

Sure I am, this is the best entertainment ever, and it's free. You don't even have to pay into the Colosseum, just turn on the TV.

Now we should be clear in our thinking—just because the price is free doesn't mean it's cost free—I'm just hoping to be dead before the butcher's bill is paid. My Capitalistic friends share many things in common, certainly mutual respect for one another, but there are other qualities and attributes that they share which I'll share with you.

First, they always mention their age in private correspondence, and they're all far older than me. They express implied happiness at being almost dead, at being at the end of their life cycle, that they won't have to live too much further into the Future. That they're almost dead is a source of personal comfort after they read, and some have written, The Philosophy of Capitalism.

Back to the Colosseum, where the predators are on stage and the prey is the audience. It's easy to become upset, though it's best not to be, there really is consolation in understanding—would you prefer false hope over entertainment? I think entertainment is the right answer.

Though the peasant doesn't choose hope over understanding; the predators are naturally manipulative while the prey have brains that are desperate—projecting their love and hope toward a messiah who'll deliver an imagined place. A place healed of depression, separatism, riots and war. Wouldn't you be desperate if your nation was dug into multiple wars? 16 years of war, it's one war a year now, with no hope of resolution.

'*Hope only serves to prolong suffering*' was Nietzsche's warning to tomorrow's peasant. Read my warning to Zero Hedgers in October: '*My contacts with The Families said Trump was being protected, that was months ago.*' It was a warning that went unheeded because hope is too addictive. Anything that causes pleasure is addictive, including hope. What's hope? It's real, it exists, within a Dream, the Dream is real.

Hope is a Dream that's infinitely better and more real than Reality. But as Reality continually contradicts the Dream their *self* resides within, frustration builds and then the peasants get mean and meaner.

That's why there are way more meaner people than nice people, that's especially true of older humans, especially men. The frustration builds up. Women are different, even a woman who has reason to be mean is nice and kind to her own children. And women appear to fantasize about their own children.

While Nietzsche analysed the future; Hegel was more concerned with the past, which revealed **fear** as the agent that drove progress toward self awareness—whereby *self* and *self-image* became the same—whereby Thought would govern the World via Reason—And so on.

Actually, I've come to realize that the limit placed upon self awareness is the absence of virtue, namely the absence of Courage. It takes Courage to deal with Reality. To see it for what it is, in its naked form.

The System is a living thing; the Natural System gives it life. And so it will seek the means to defend itself. It will develop an immune system so to speak; to reject burdens and critiques. Of course it also has instruments to defend itself; the System was designed to serve the Dominant Class who protect it consciously. And then there is Instinct—Any individual who depends upon the System for his survival will defend it instinctively.

Now this Instinct is shared by all insiders so it operates as a force at the System Level—this force is exclusive and seeks to ostracise and make powerless any threats to continuity, e.g. the unemployed, or any nation that favours Gold over the FIAT, that prefers publicly to privately owned banks.

The insiders' *thinking will* is aborted as the power of belief, and conformity of thought, is required to oppress and demoralize outsiders. The power to suppress any doubt about sustainability or the fairness of outcomes is called for. *"Those people are homeless due to their weak character"* so to speak, or *"The Middle East is a mess because they're inbred."* Pat Buchanan rails against immigrants, after his friends spent decades making money from desperate labour—demoralised first and then displaced by death squads sent by us, the Dominant Class—to kill anyone trying to make Central America a liveable place. Duplicity and delusion are the handmaidens of success in the business of peasant-debt-slave manipulation, right? And that's not a critique, the status quo has served me well, so thanks Pat.

So there's no critical thinking at the System Level by those benefiting from the System—though there is feeling; Liberals are prone to guilt for example, and now the retards are ashamed for falling for the appearance of nationalism— This protective Instinct drives the evolution of myth, fantasy, belief and social peer pressure that serves to prolong the System.

Another thing I've noted about my friends is that they don't care about other people, they're respectively capital- or empire-centric, and anyone who's not human-centric is ultimately anti-human. I came to this realisation after publishing a post entitled 'Capitalism Causes us to be Mentally Ill' and no one read it. Visitors to my site are almost all capitalists, I know this since I can track what site they've come from—FT, Zero Hedge mostly—and they also write me. And they refuse to write reviews about our books because they don't care about society or other readers. It's almost funny for me; but you need to be mean to remain Dominant, right? So no hard feelings between me and my friends.

Not so much fun for the masses who assumed Trump cared about them. Trump is a Capitalist so he is Capital-centric, thus he doesn't care about people. But try explaining that to a peasant.

The Fed's sole mandate is not to help Americans (people) but to protect and preserve the System, which is demonstrably true given recent behaviour. What about the Bank of England? How many Billions is it printing every day? Does any insider care to count? Or check? Or dare to question?

As Marx realised from his studies; it's hard to change the System. He realised the need for Revolution—the wholesale transformation of society by killing those at the Top who benefit from the System.

His fantasy failed; and interestingly, we also know why.

The System is profit and consumer-centric. But if you can't consume, then you don't exist, do you?

During a recent debate about the carrying capacity of the planet I mentioned to an American capitalist that there are 7 billion people and he corrected me, correctly. He was leery of the 7 billion figure since many Africans don't really consume, and so they don't really exist within the System.

Capitalists live in their own fantasy but my friends chose to deal with Reality. That's why I respect them, they have Courage.

So what does Reality look like?

There's no one in control. The System will continue until it kills everyone. Extinction is the System Result.

You want facts to explicitly substantiate that statement? Sure, that's easy for me. The System Framework requires incremental growth in commodity inputs and consumption both serve to validate the creation of interest bearing debt; the interest is profit—which becomes income for my friends at the top of the Dominant Class.

Incremental Growth in commodity inputs—the result is Depletion. Which calls for wars of aggression, and annihilation. The nukes keep the peace, for now, but they also mean the next big war carries risk of extinction.

So how to change the System? How to manufacture mass desire for a change of the System framework? And such change, is it worthwhile?

At the very minimum; change would require pain on a biblical scale. It takes pain to de-condition the brain, it's what Pavlov taught us.

One of the often unstated benefits of a First Strike against Russia is that 3 to 4 billion would die from crop failure alone. That's a lot of pain. And then there's The Reset—the other option—it can be managed in such a way as to depopulate entire regions. That also carries the risk of extinction.

If The Reset happens and cosmic numbers start starving—then I can guarantee you this—it's not an accident.

The Fed chairs are terrified and have been for some time, so they know. Actually, unlike the old farts you see on TV, I personally don't criticize anyone, I think the Fed chairs have done a good job. They prolonged a System that wasn't designed to be permanent. And the people who criticize them, for lying, are being a little disingenuous. If they told the truth there'd be a panic and then billions would suffer.

You'll note the critics always have a plan for that part of the System which they think is broken, but in general, you'll note no specifics. You'll note they are unable to criticize my output, look around, where's the criticism? No criticism! Because they can't imagine at the System Level. No way to get from Here to their Fantasy. And they know it.

For example, the Central Banks are criticised for picking winners—for direct funding of particular companies—but the critics fail to provide an alternative approach. Here's a nugget of truth to chew on:

The System is deflating. The economy is now a negative sum game. Sure, some companies continue to run at a financial profit and others at a financial loss—all the balance sheets will always balance out. But, it no longer matters if you invest in a company that runs at a profit because the rate of return will, almost always, be below the rate of inflation. This is because the System is deflating and the amount of money in circulation is always increasing.

Try to see it this way: Imagine all value is hot air that's stored in a balloon. A portion of the air is being consumed continually so the balloon wants to deflate. The real economy must continually take inputs from the Natural System and blow hot air into the balloon. If the balloon is inflated by 2%, then the average rate of return on all investments will be 2%.

Now there are less inputs so there is less hot air and the balloon is deflating. You can still invest, and your company may run at a profit; you may even get a dividend, and then you sell your shares. But it doesn't matter because the money returned to you will have less purchasing power than the money you invested. The balloon has deflated so there's less value for sale. So there's ever more money competing for ever less value.

The significance of such cannot be overstated. If this were understood by the masses no new companies would be formed. Capital injections into all going concerns would cease. Why would any person risk his privately owned wealth in any enterprise when the returned monies would buy less value than they presently do? You'd be better off buying Gold or using your working capital to reduce your cost of living, i.e. become self-sufficient.

For example, insulating a poorly insulated attic in a typical house will pay for itself in 3 years in energy savings. That's a 33% rate of return, tax and risk free. For an uninsulated basement the payback is about 5 years but that's still a 20% tax and risk free rate of return. Compare that to negative interest rates in a bank account plus inflation plus fees, or the extreme risk that markets are offering right now. Energy conservation is, by far, the best investment there is. **There's no point in playing a negative sum game, so avoid it if you can.**

The take-away from the last few chapters is singular: you need to protect the company. If they go under, en masse, then it's anarchy. The market will unravel And a lot of knowledge will be lost. Together, these carry significant risk of extinction: The cities would ignite almost instantly. The neatest long term solution is to hand over ownership of the company to the present management and workforce. They'll continue to labour for additional income.

Some companies will continue to run at a financial loss and will need bond buying support by the Mint. An interest rate of say 4% would bankrupt poorly performing companies in a timely fashion and liquidate their assets with minimal cost to society. Start-ups with patented technology will require 100% direct financing by the Mint until a given cut-off point. The population proper will require a Universal Basic Income, also provided by the Mint, as only 20% of the population will be required for production, due to ever more automation.

You may think this solution is extraordinary or bizarre. But it already IS the solution: The top Central Bankers know what the problem is and they're already doing the only thing they can do. That is, holding the market together by financing companies running at a loss—"as of the latest data, central banks own just over a third of the global tradable bond universe of $54 trillion, or roughly $18 trillion."

Usury is no longer called for as there is no more growth. The actual stable solution is lawful money issued into the commons, as intended by the Founding Fathers of the United States of America. Lawful money is the fiat of the people, not of bankers. The usurpation of the Law and of the commons by usury needs to be undone by changing money to become legal fiat.

As soon as it is stamped with some sort of exchange value money becomes fiat. We haven't used metal by weight since many thousands of years ago in the Ancient Near East, and even then it related to temple ledgers, which were denominated in barley.

These monies supplied by the Mint will be the money of the people and the prices of all goods and services supplied by the people will inflate to match the fiat in circulation. It really is that simple.

Without this framework change the companies will fail, and we will die. The high-tech facilities which store nuclear materials require stable supply.

With respect to the sociopath problem:

The solution is institutionalized decentralisation: Direct democracy and public offices allocated by lottery. Crypto-currencies will undermine the re-growth of a usury-driven-system to keep your savings safe—Gold may be out of reach after The Reset. "Saving" shouldn't be much of a problem going forward because there'll be very little to "save." The problem of pensions and savings is more fundamental than many imagine: how do you "save" when almost all assets depreciate due to entropy? When bankers use the word "save" it just means they take your money (aka unconsumed value) and give it to some risk taker willing to gamble it against chance and entropy.

In a deflating system the sum of all inputs is decreasing—thus, the sum of all value produced and consumed is decreasing—thus, growth is negative—thus, no interest on your savings is possible—the result is no system or way of financially "growing savings" for society. You can still give your "savings" to a bank and they'll try to give it to a risk taker, but the money returned will almost always have less buying power due to entropy of existing assets and a deflating system with more money.

All that is required for civilisation is an equitable distribution of production, buying power, land, and the working hours required to keep the market moving. Land is unusual as it's fixed in supply and so can be hoarded and price-fixed by Oligarchs.

Our situation is worse than the Middle Ages, when the economy was a zero sum game with no growth. Our situation is negative for the foreseeable future. So History cannot be our guide. With understanding comes a degree of control. And what do we understand? We understand that the System is completely dead and defunct. Usury demands that the future is more productive than the present: *Essentially, the additional real product has been* **sold to the lender** *who has deferred collection. And in the form of interest is promised a payment for that deferral by the borrower.* Capitalism shall end with The Families collecting what is legally theirs. There'll be no more Capital accumulated so the Age of Capital has passed.

The Reset will be to Prices.

What will the next Age be like? Or is this the last Age? These questions are intriguing. Why is it that we're now aware of what's gone wrong, before the collapse, and also why only a handful can prepare properly for it?

All this makes me wonder about God (the Absolute) and von Hartmann's output during the 19th century. I read it as a youngster and it has always stayed with me.

According to von Hartmann the unconscious Absolute (God) is both will and idea, which respectively account for the existence of the world and its orderly nature. Will appears in suffering, idea in order and consciousness. Thus there are grounds for both pessimism and optimism, and, since the Absolute is one, these must be reconciled. As the cosmic process advances, whereby the Mind comes to know Itself via knowledge accumulation, idea prevails over will, making possible aesthetic and intellectual pleasures.

But intellectual development increases our capacity for pain, and material progress suppresses spiritual values. Hence ultimate happiness is not attainable in this world, in heaven, or by endless progress towards an earthly paradise.

The illusions of progress are ruses employed by the Absolute to induce mankind to propagate itself. To keep having children. We will eventually shed illusions and commit collective suicide—the final, redeeming triumph of idea over will, of reason over lust, of knowledge over hope. The idea has created thermonuclear weapons which increasingly impede the will to kill, rob and rape. Though eventually, the will, will act.

Imperialism and Capitalism produced an abnormal growth in the species—one which is anti-human. They are evil. Their first function and reason for existence is to create unequal power relations between humans—Inequality and powerlessness for the average man. The evil ones want power to satisfy sadistic urges in the unconscious, e.g. paedophilia, torture, sex and slavery. Religion is held together by pure will to power and co-dependency. See the dynamic between Margaret Thatcher, Pinochet and Jimmy Savile to see power-centric evil in action.

Religion is about power. One must forgo power to become separate. The *separate self* has no power and is treated to contempt by the true believers.

The cosmic process continues to bring humans closer to AI. And this delivers a new source of optimism. Once the desire for power is discarded, one can discard pessimism about mankind, and attain Understanding:

God created the cosmic process and is the centre of all things.

The End

of

The Philosophy of Capitalism

by

Putrid

5ᵗʰ Edition

Copyright © 2017 Cathal Haughian
All rights reserved.

This book is presented solely for educational purposes. The author and publisher are not offering it as financial, economic, or other professional services advice. Neither the author nor the publisher shall be held liable or responsible to any person or entity with respect to any loss or incidental or consequential damages caused, or alleged to have been caused, directly or indirectly, by the information or programs contained herein.

The names of the characters and contributors referred to in this book are fictional. All content providers use pseudonyms. Any likeness to actual persons, either living or dead, is strictly coincidental. The author and publisher have no relationship with The Financial Times, The Pearson Group or Nihon Keizai Shimbun (Nikkei).

Made in the USA
Lexington, KY
14 August 2017